PREPARING FOR ORGANIZATIONAL TRANSFORMATION

Harold M. Schroeder

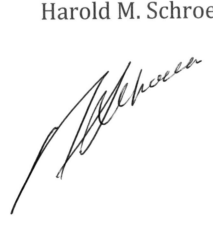

Copyright © 2016 Harold M. Schroeder
All rights reserved.
ISBN-10: 153086691X
ISBN-13: 978-1530866915

Library of Congress Control Number: 2016906303
CreateSpace Independent Publishing Platform, North Charleston, SC

DEDICATION

To my family and friends.

CONTENTS

Executive Summary	7
Introduction	11
The Importance and Risks of Transformation	15
The Nature and Characteristics of Transformation	23
The Importance of Art and Science	41
The Executive Sponsor / Project Manager Partnership	55
Transformation – the Role of the Project Manager	67
Transformation – the Role of the Executive Sponsor	99
Transformation Assessment Systems and Tools	129
Summary and Conclusion	137
References	141

EXECUTIVE SUMMARY

Organizations of all types now regularly have to implement major change initiatives in order to survive and remain competitive in the face of new challenges and economic pressures. Some key drivers of organizational transformation that have become especially important in recent years include economic uncertainty, intensified business competition, advances in information and communications technology, and new and emerging business models.

The costs and business risks of these major organizational transformations are often very high, yet the importance of advance preparation for an organizational change initiative is often neglected. Further, there is a widespread lack of understanding among business executives about exactly what is required to properly prepare.

In particular, the nature of transformation projects now demands very different types of project management skills than in the past, with a shift away from primarily technical project management and towards the need for an understanding of the business environment and skillful stakeholder management.

However, major change projects are almost always risky, and organizational transformations have become increasingly complex and challenging. A large body of research evidence indicates that organizational transformation projects have high failure rates. Many transformations are terminated before completion or fail to deliver the intended benefits within the agreed time and budget, often at high cost to the organizations concerned.

We have found in particular that, when projects go wrong, this is most often due to the failure to implement what we refer to as an "art- and science"-based approach to transformation. In this framework, we conceptualize the "science" of transformation as the formal project management techniques, methods and tools that PMBOK® focuses on and other project management standards. We define the "art" of transformation as the more intangible or intuitive skills and attributes that are important in managing the people-related aspects of change and the strategic and business development aspects of transformation project management. In any transformation project, it is crucial to achieve the right combination of art and science.

Transformations also often fail, we contend, because organizational leaders fail to understand that effective transformation means consistently focusing on the organization's fundamental purpose and core values while undergoing the organizational changes that are necessary to pursue these differently over time. In the book, we explain this more fully and highlight why an art and science approach is essential for planning and implementing effective transformations that can deliver the intended business results.

In particular, we focus on the respective roles of the Project Manager and the Executive Sponsor, the two key players in any transformation initiative. We describe the nature of the Executive Sponsor/Project Manager partnership and explain why this has become such a critical success factor in organizational transformation. Then we examine the specific responsibilities of each of these key players in transformation, and the types of art and science skills needed to perform their roles successfully. In particular, we identify five important skill "clusters" in the art of transformation project management for the new business environment. We also identify and explain three crucial roles of the Executive Sponsor: preparing the organization for an "art- and science"-based transformation, project governance and ensuring the organization can achieve its strategic transformation objectives. In the final chapter of the book, we provide examples of three practical tools for evaluating and improving an organization's readiness to undergo a successful transformation.

INTRODUCTION

As Benjamin Franklin said, "By failing to prepare, you are preparing to fail."

Traditionally, organizational change tended to be incremental or small-scale in nature and often confined to a single department or functional area (Burke, 2010). This situation is changing dramatically. In recent years, a new environment has been evolving in which frequent or on-going organizational change and whole-enterprise transformations are becoming the norm rather than the exception.

Organizations of all types now regularly have to implement major change initiatives in order to survive and remain competitive in the face of new challenges and economic pressures. Some key drivers of organizational transformation that have become especially important in recent years include economic uncertainty, intensified business competition, advances in information and communications technology and emerging new business models, factors that we explore in more detail in Chapter 2.

Organizational transformations take many different forms but include:

- Implementation of a new business strategy

PREPARING FOR ORGANIZATIONAL TRANSFORMATION

- Transformation to support a major new service or product launch
- Cross-organizational IT system implementation
- Organizational streamlining or downsizing
- Post-merger integration

It is now common for major transformation initiatives to involve all areas of an organization, as well as external stakeholders, as companies increasingly come to recognize the inter-relatedness of their mission, strategy, leadership and culture and the need for a holistic approach to change. In this context, the individuals responsible for overseeing and managing such projects play a crucial role in the ability of the organization to meet its strategic goals.

The costs and business risks of these major organizational transformations are often very high, yet the importance of advance preparation for an organizational change initiative is often neglected. Furthermore, there is a widespread lack of understanding among business executives about what is required to properly prepare.

In particular, the nature of transformation projects now demands very different types of project management skills than in the past, with a shift away from primarily technical project management and towards the need for an understanding of the business and for skillful stakeholder management.

This book aims to provide organizational leaders with an understanding of the importance of transformation and how to prepare for this so that a successful transformation that delivers the intended business benefits can be achieved. In particular, the book focuses on the respective roles of the Project Manager and the Executive Sponsor, the two key players in any transformation initiative, and identifies the types of skills needed to perform these roles successfully.

Our approach is based on a recommended Art and Science of Transformation® framework, developed by Schroeder & Schroeder

INTRODUCTION

Inc. It reflects an extensive review of the organizational change literature; many surveys of Board Members, Executives, and Project Managers involved in organizational transformation initiatives; as well as more than thirty years' experience of helping organizations of all types and sizes to successfully transform.

This framework will help organizations understand the nature of successful transformation and achieve an appropriate balance in transformation management between technical project management skills and the business-related and interpersonal skills that have become so important.

We then examine the roles of the two key players in this process: the transformation Project Manager and the project's Executive project Sponsor, and identify the specific types of art and science skills that the individuals in these roles need to have, emphasizing the need to combine art and science in different areas of project management.

The remainder of the book is organized as follows:

- In Chapter 2 we examine the reasons why frequent and major organizational transformation has become important in today's business environment and highlight the risks and costs of transformation failure.
- In Chapter 3 we examine the ways in which organizational transformation projects differ from more traditional change initiatives, and what types of new skills and expertise are needed to ensure their success. We look in more detail at the reasons why transformation projects often fail and provide an overview of our recommended Art and Science of Transformation® approach.
- In Chapter 4, we explore what constitutes effective organizational transformation, and how the Art and Science of Transformation® framework can be used to explain this. Some critical success factors are identified that organizations must address in order to successfully transform.

- Chapter 5 discusses the critical partnership between the Executive Sponsor and the Project Manager of a transformation initiative, identifying the key roles and responsibilities involved, and the ways in which these are interrelated.
- Chapter 6 focuses on the role and responsibilities of the Project Manager and discusses, in particular, the importance of effectively managing the high-performance transformation team and ensuring that the project can achieve its operational objectives. We also identify the key art and science skills needed to perform these roles.
- Chapter 7 focuses on the main roles of the Executive Sponsor: preparing the organization for successful transformation; implementing effective project governance and ensuring the organization can meet its strategic transformation objectives. We also identify the key art and science skills required in these roles.
- Chapter 8 provides some practical examples of transformation readiness assessment tools that can be adapted for use by different organizations to help identify how to improve their transformation performance.

Finally, we summarize the key messages of the book and provide links for further advice and assistance in transformation project management.

THE IMPORTANCE AND RISKS OF TRANSFORMATION

As highlighted in Chapter 1, today's business environment is rapidly changing, requiring organizations of all types and sizes to continually transform in order to achieve business growth and meet their goals. Many business researchers now argue that continuous change and innovation are essential if organizations are to remain competitive and efficient (Jugdey & Mathur, 2012; Savoleinen, 2013; Zekic & Samarzija, 2012). As a result, major organizational change initiatives are becoming the norm rather than the exception for many organizations.

The need for frequent transformation is not confined to the private sector. Governmental and other non-profit entities are also forced to continually evaluate and improve how they work in order to cope with budget squeezes and increased accountability, serve their customers better and pursue their missions most effectively (Datt & Nash, 2013; Kaplan, 2012).

In this chapter, we identify some of the main drivers of change, to help explain why regular transformation is becoming a necessity for many organizations. We draw on the findings of international employer surveys to demonstrate the frequency of organizational change in this environment, including the project rates and associated costs, which highlight the risks and challenges that are often faced when implementing organizational change initiatives.

DRIVERS OF ORGANIZATIONAL TRANSFORMATION

Some key drivers of organizational transformation that have become especially important include economic uncertainty, intensified business competition, advances in information and communications technology, and new and emerging business models.

Drawing on statistics and information collected by other researchers, seven key drivers of organizational transformation are identified and discussed below.

1. Economic pressures and uncertainty:
 - In recent years, the business environment has been changing dramatically. The global economic crisis of the late 2000s has left a legacy of continuing economic pressure and uncertainty for many firms in what is sometimes referred to as the "new normal".
 - Organizations now need to continually seek ways of reducing costs and improving efficiencies, especially in the face of severe competition from home and abroad.

2. Globalization of activity:
 - Continuing globalization of economic activity exacerbates these pressures, as overseas competitors are often able to deliver comparable products and

- services at significantly lower cost than Western countries.
- The McKinsey Global Institute recently reported that the global flow of goods and services has recovered from the recession and has now "surpassed their 2007 peak" (McKinsey Global Institute, 2014).
- In this context, it is perhaps unsurprising that a recent survey of CEOs in the U.S. found that 60% are concerned about competition from new entrants in their markets (PricewaterhouseCoopers, 2014).

3. New forms of employment:

- The ways in which economic activity is organized have also been radically changing, due to developments in information and communications technology, coupled with the economic pressures and resulting need to reduce staffing costs.
- Instead of taking on permanent employees, firms are increasingly recruiting contract-based workers: one study has predicted that more than 50% of all workers in the U.S. will be non-permanent staff by 2020 (MBO Partners, 2011).
- Organizations are also taking advantage of technology to create geographically dispersed virtual teams which sometimes span the globe. This

	is not only to reduce costs but to access valuable skills and expertise that might be unavailable or too expensive to secure locally.
4. Increased emphasis on innovation:	▪ At the same time, companies are drawing on rapidly changing technologies to become more innovative, responding to highly competitive markets by introducing a flow of new products and services or continually improving existing product lines.
5. Use of technology to improve business processes:	▪ The increased reliance on information technology as just one technological business tool is reflected in high levels of spending in this area, expected to reach $3.8 trillion worldwide in 2014 according to a recent business report (Gartner, 2013).
6. Social media and the changing nature of business relationships:	▪ With the growth in the use of the Internet and social media, direct communication with vast networks of individuals and organizations has become relatively easy. However, it is only those firms that are able to successfully cultivate trust-based brands and relationships in this environment, who truly have a competitive advantage. This involves a whole new business paradigm, often requiring extensive changes in corporate culture as well as systems.

THE IMPORTANCE AND RISKS OF TRANSFORMATION

7. Regulatory compliance requirements:

- Last but not least, organizations increasingly have to operate within a much tighter regulatory environment than in the past and ensure that they are fully compliant with applicable regulations and reporting requirements in multiple areas including health and safety, employment, finance, the environment and human rights.

- In the U.S., one tangible sign of this development has been a massive 122% increase in private-sector compliance staff between 2009 and 2012, a trend which is expected to increase as more than 500 additional regulations are introduced in the near future (Batkins, 2013).

TRANSFORMATION STATISTICS

The impacts of these drivers of change are reflected in the results of business surveys and other studies that have highlighted the frequency of organizational transformation initiatives in recent years, and the magnitude of such projects. For example:

- In 2007, 86% of senior executives who responded to a survey of major European corporations said that business transformation had become a central way of working in their organization and, on average, the companies surveyed reported carrying out seven major transformations in the previous three years (Cap Gemini, 2007).
- In a 2009 CapGemini Consulting survey of more than 300 large European companies, 82% of respondents indicated that transformation is of vital importance to their business, and reported that they typically instigate at least two

- organizational change projects every year.
- The Project Management Institute (2011) reported that organizations are conducting increasingly large and more complex "high stakes" projects with an average budget of U.S.$4.4 million.

TRANSFORMATION FAILURE RATES

Major change projects are almost always risky, however, and organizational transformations have become increasingly complex and challenging. There is considerable evidence from business surveys that many organizations struggle with these change initiatives. For example:

- Only 30% of respondents in the Cap Gemini 2007 survey of European executives indicated that their company was excelling at business transformation.
- The PMI Pulse of the Profession study (2014) found that just 9% of organizations surveyed regarded themselves as excellent on executing initiatives to deliver strategic results.

Perhaps even more worrying, a large body of research evidence indicates that organizational transformation projects have high rates of failure.

Many transformations are reportedly terminated before completion or fail to deliver the intended benefits within the agreed time and budget, often at high cost to the organizations concerned.

- PricewaterhouseCoopers analyzed 10,640 projects from 200 companies internationally and found evidence that only 2.5% were successfully completed (cited in Hardy-Vallee, 2012).
- Analysis of thirteen case studies of different types of business transformations conducted in major European corporations found that only 30% were deemed to have been successful and 40% only partly successful, while the remaining 30% had failed completely, often at great cost to

their organizations (Ward & Uhl, 2012).
- In a 2008 survey by the Economist Intelligence Unit, 58% of senior business Executive respondents said that more than half of their change initiatives over the previous five years had not been successful.
- IBM (2008) reported similar results from research with more than 1,500 Project Managers worldwide, who indicated that only 41% of their change initiatives had been successful in meeting their time, budget and quality objectives (IBM, 2008).
- Based on a survey of more than 200 organizations in a range of sectors, KPMG New Zealand found evidence that organizational project success rates had declined in recent years. In 2012, only 29% of respondents reported that their projects had consistently been delivered on time, only 33% on budget and only 35% on scope.
- According to PMI's Pulse of the Profession report (2014), only 56% of strategic initiatives meet their original goals and business intent. As a result, it was estimated by PMI that organizations lose $109 million for every $1 billion invested in projects and programs (PMI, 2014).
- One source reports that 39% of U.S. projects with budgets over $5 million fail (cited in Business Reporter, 2013).

Added to the direct financial losses involved in project failure are the negative impacts on staff morale, not to mention the indirect costs of organizational disruption during the change initiative.

- A study of 5,400 major IT projects with budgets over $15 million found that 17% went so badly wrong that they threatened the existence of the organization itself (Bloch, Blumberg & Laartz, 2012).
- In the UK, it was reported that an aborted IT system implementation for the National Health Service cost the government £10 billion (The Guardian, September 18, 2013).

Why do Transformation Projects Fail?

The symptoms of a failing project will be all too familiar to many readers: running behind schedule or going over budget; accusations and finger-pointing between the project team and other groups within the organization; the various stakeholders giving out very different messages about project progress ... the list goes on. So why is it that so many organizational transformation projects go wrong?

Based on research and practical experience of helping numerous organizations transform, we have found that the importance of advance preparation for an organizational change initiative is often neglected, and there is a widespread lack of awareness among business executives about what is required to properly prepare. Indeed, there is a lack of understanding about what constitutes successful organizational transformation, why it is necessary and how to achieve it.

We have found in particular that, when projects go wrong, it is most often due to the failure to adopt what we refer to as an "art and science"-based approach to transformation. This approach has, we believe, become a critical success factor in organizational change due to developments in the business environment and the changing nature of transformation projects. We explain this further in Chapters 3 and 4, first exploring what constitutes a successful transformation. Here, we examine the ways in which transformation projects are becoming more complex and requiring new forms of project management expertise and we set out our recommended Art and Science of Transformation® framework.

THE NATURE AND CHARACTERISTICS OF TRANSFORMATION

In this chapter, we begin to set out a case for a new type of "art- and science"-based transformation project management to meet the needs of today's organizations..

In order to do so:

- We discuss what constitutes effective organizational transformation and why it is necessary; defining transformation as the changes needed to ensure a firm can most effectively achieve its core purpose and goals, given the opportunities and risks inherent in the current business environment.
- We identify some specific characteristics of transformation projects that make them different from other types of projects with more narrowly defined objectives, and which require a whole new approach to project management.

WHAT IS EFFECTIVE ORGANIZATIONAL TRANSFORMATION?

By definition, transformation implies radical, all-embracing organizational changes as opposed to more modest ones. Organizational transformations take a wide range of forms depending on the reason for undertaking them and the desired business goals, but some common examples include:

- Organizational streamlining/downsizing
- Merger integration
- Strategy implementation
- IT system implementation
- New service, program or product launch

Organizational transformations of these types are generally large scale and complex; they directly involve the whole organization and often multiple external organizations, and are mission-critical in nature.

Anderson & Anderson (2013) distinguish transformational change from "transitional projects" which can be implemented using traditional change management approaches. They characterize transformations by the high degree of uncertainty about the future state and how exactly to get there and an intended outcome that will be so very different that the people and culture of the organization must change their very mindsets and behaviours for it to be achieved.

Readers may quite reasonably be wondering why such extensive transformation projects are necessary, given the likely costs of such extensive change, the high level of organizational disruption involved and the inherent risks of failure.

In this chapter, we explain why a strategic and holistic approach to transformation is crucial to success. We define effective transformation as being:

1. Concerned with enabling the organization to achieve its core purpose through the defined strategic objectives, and
2. Holistic in nature, involving all areas and aspects of the organization including its people, culture, systems and processes.

THE NATURE AND CHARACTERISTICS OF TRANSFORMATION

In the following section, we explain what effective transformation consists of, and go on to discuss the importance of a holistic approach to organizational transformation, highlighting the linkages between different organizational components and the importance of ensuring they are aligned in order to promote rather than hinder successful change.

THE ROLE OF FUNDAMENTAL PURPOSE AND CORE VALUES

Effective transformation, we contend, means consistently focusing on the organization's fundamental purpose and core values, while undergoing the organizational changes that are necessary to pursue these differently over time in behavioural and product/service terms.

This approach ensures that the firm retains its basic character and most importantly provides direction and stability over time while undertaking transformation projects that enable it to pursue its purpose most effectively in the prevailing environment.

Strategic transformation often becomes necessary because changes in the external environment threaten the organization's competitive position and there is a need for realignment through a major change process.

This typically involves adopting new strategies, products or ways of operating that enable the firm to position itself most appropriately in the new environment to effectively pursue its fundamental purpose. The purpose itself should remain unchanged.

For this reason, organizational change initiatives need to be properly planned and implemented within the company's core strategic planning processes as shown in Figure 1, with fundamental purpose and core values as the guiding principles. This will often result in increased awareness of the need for transformative change, rather than a tweaking of existing approaches.

Figure 1: The Strategic Transformation Planning Process

Projects that are not planned and executed in this way have considerably higher failure rates.

PMI (2014) report that 71% of projects that are aligned with an organization's strategy are completed successfully, compared with just 48% of those that are misaligned with the strategy.

As observed by Collins & Porras (2005), Core Values and Fundamental Purpose represent the essence and very identity of an organization, and should be regarded as its "guiding principles" which influence all that the organization does. A consistent focus on Core Values and Fundamental Purpose ensures that the firm retains its basic character over time, providing direction and stability in an often-turbulent external environment.

The links between a company's fundamental purpose and values and its business performance are well supported by the findings of empirical research. Collins & Porras (2005) tracked the stock market performance of firms since 1925 and found that companies such as Disney and Boeing, which have retained a consistent purpose and values while modifying their specific strategies and products over time, have significantly outperformed their competitors on many business performance measures.

THE NATURE AND CHARACTERISTICS OF TRANSFORMATION

The benefits are not just financial: a clear focus on purpose and values enables a firm to build better relationships with customers and other organizations, attract and retain high-quality employees and improve its innovation performance, as documented in many research studies (e.g. Collins, 1995; Denning, 2012; Lory & McCalman, 2002; Thornbury, 2003; Vandermerwe, 2004).

Defined and used correctly, a firm's Fundamental Purpose and Core Values differentiate it from competitors and provide a focus of identity and "relate-ability" for employees and customers alike. This potentially results in a range of business benefits including more effective team working, higher sales and increased brand loyalty.

DEFINING FUNDAMENTAL PURPOSE AND CORE VALUES

The challenge for many organizations, however, is how to properly identify and communicate their fundamental purpose so that it becomes an effective business tool that remains relevant and useful over time. Purpose is perhaps most often thought of in terms of generating revenue or supplying particular types of products and services and, in a misguided approach, firms focus on making limited changes through new product lines with the objective of increasing profits (Taylor, 2013). When they take this approach, and external market conditions change, a lack of direction and focus can result and the company's fundamental identity can be weakened.

Instead, we contend that fundamental purpose should always be defined in terms of the human needs and combinations of needs that the organization is ultimately concerned with meeting. All organizations have basically been established to address specific human needs, and the main categories into which these fall are universal and unchanging. Even those organizations providing products or services to other businesses are simply part of a chain established to satisfy the various needs of humanity.

For example, in response to customer preferences, many firms are concerned with providing products that address a basic human need for nutrition or for transportation, combined with a higher-level demand for comfort or luxury. This is a simplistic example; in practice, it is the unique ways in which firms address more complex combinations of needs and demands that enable them to effectively differentiate their brand and compete effectively for customers in a particular market niche.

While fundamental purpose should remain the same over time, organizational transformation is important to ensure that a company adapts to the prevailing business environment in its efforts to satisfy human needs, especially the additional higher-level needs which often change according to current fashions, trends and economic circumstances.

A useful tool for understanding fundamental purpose in people-related terms is Maslow's Hierarchy of Needs framework, originally developed to explain individual motivation. Maslow argued that all human activity is motivated by the desire to fulfill particular types of needs, which he conceptualized as falling into the categories shown in Figure 2 and described below.

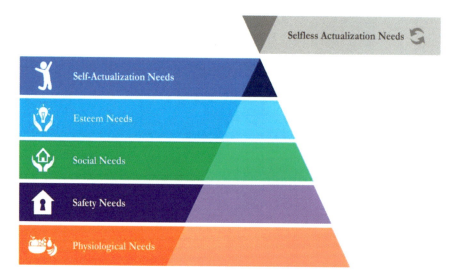

Figure 2: Using Maslow's Hierarchy of Needs to determine fundamental purpose

- Physiological Needs: The most basic level consists of physiological needs needed to sustain human life, such as air, water, food and shelter.
- Safety Needs: Once their basic physiological needs are met, Maslow argued, humans turn their focus to ensuring their physical safety as well their economic or financial security, for example by securing employment.
- Social Needs: The next level identified by Maslow is the need for social interaction with other humans, both in the work and personal contexts. Humans are basically social creatures and form relationships with one another to fulfill social needs and to work collectively towards business objectives that cannot be met in isolation.
- Esteem Needs: Humans have a higher-level need for recognition and respect from others, which they become motivated to achieve once their lower-level needs are fulfilled. Also referred to by Maslow as "ego", the need for self-esteem can be satisfied by achieving control or authority over other people, or through recognition for personal achievements.
- Self-Actualization Needs: While the four previous levels of human needs were defined by Maslow as deficiency needs, the fifth level was defined as a "growth" need, in which people are no longer concerned with meeting deficiencies but are focused on self-improvement and fulfilling one's full potential through personal and spiritual growth experiences.
- In a later (posthumous) publication (1971) Maslow identified a further level, defined as "beyond self-actualization", in which individuals are finally motivated not by self- interest but by selfless needs or by a calling to serve the needs of humanity more generally. Greene & Burke (2007) have defined this level as "selfless-actualization".

Organizations also fulfill various levels of human needs among their own employees through the pursuit of their fundamental purpose, and the effectiveness with which they are able to do so largely influences their overall business performance.

For example, though individuals may join organizations primarily to make a living, once this basic need is satisfied they look to their jobs for the satisfaction of other needs such as social interaction with others, the chance to develop new skills and especially the opportunity for meaningful work that serves a higher purpose (Holbeche, 2006; Pink, 2009). If employees perceive that the organization meets their needs in these ways, they are more likely to be motivated to work hard and efficiently in pursuit of the fundamental purpose of the company (Rieches, 2010).

An organization's Core Values are also very important in contributing to its strategic focus. This is because the Core Values underpin the types of choices that are made about how to interact with the external world, including acceptable and desirable ways of interacting with customers, the relative emphasis on social as opposed to purely economic goals, and so on. Core values might include, for example, a focus on collaboration and teamwork, putting the customer first, honesty and integrity or product excellence.

Overall, the values and the choices they lead to will help to determine the market position adopted by the firm. Core values also often go unacknowledged in the planning process, resulting in failed initiatives when directions are pursued that are in conflict with these values and fail to engage organizational members or attract customers.

THE NEED FOR A HOLISTIC APPROACH

TRANSFORMING CULTURE

Another common reason for transformation project failure is not recognizing the inter-relationships between different parts of the organization. Project failures are common, for example, when firms attempt to introduce a new business strategy or working practice without recognizing that the corporate culture has developed in a

THE NATURE AND CHARACTERISTICS OF TRANSFORMATION

symbiotic fashion with the existing strategy and ways of doing things.

Moreover, while individual resistance to change can sometimes be easily overcome by effectively communicating the benefits of the initiative, corporate culture can present a more intractable barrier that reinforces existing ways of thinking and behaving in the workplace, and proactive measures are, therefore, necessary to promote culture change.

Organizational culture basically consists of the core values, norms and acceptable or expected behaviours that influence how people go about their jobs and interact with one another in that particular workplace. While core values represent the essence of an organization's being and ideally remain constant over time, norms and behaviours are the aspects of organizational culture that must be reviewed and reshaped as necessary to ensure they support the desired strategy and goals.

Norms can be defined as the informal "rules" which govern patterns of behaviours and interaction among organizational members. Behaviours are the outward manifestation of organizational culture, through which values and norms are expressed in actions that have a direct impact on the achievement of goals. The objective of cultural change is to adapt norms and behaviours, within the scope of the organization's core values, to bring these into alignment with a new business strategy or direction.

At the individual level, effective communication of the proposed transformation initiative to all employees is important to create initial awareness and eventual understanding of the desired changes. The new business strategy or other changes must be communicated clearly to staff throughout the organization using a range of formal and informal methods and in ways that are tailored to their information needs and perspectives.

But communication alone is rarely sufficient to bring about the necessary changes in norms and behaviours: employees also need to

PREPARING FOR ORGANIZATIONAL TRANSFORMATION

be involved more actively and directly in the transformation initiative. Team meetings, staff workshops or other forums should, therefore, be used to involve employees directly in translating the new strategy or goals to their own areas of work.

There is a clear five-stage process of behavioural change in which individuals gain awareness and understanding of a new initiative, translate this understanding to their own situation, and gradually become committed to and internalize the changes (Figure 3).

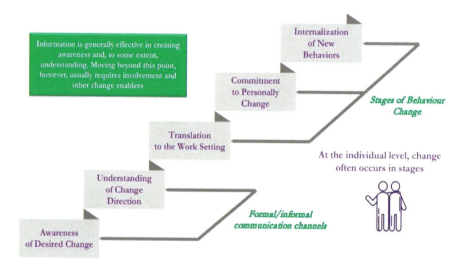

Figure 3: The stages of Employee-level Cultural Transformation

CULTURAL CHANGE-SHAPING LEVERS

It is also crucial to recognize that corporate culture becomes institutionalized and ingrained in the very fabric of the organization, shaping its structure and systems and, in turn, being reinforced by these.

In particular, seven of these "change-shaping levers" can be identified that can either facilitate or act as barriers to successful transformation, by enabling the organization to secure particular types of skills or by promoting or discouraging certain types of behaviour among organizational members. These are shown in

Figure 4 and explained below.

Figure 4: Cultural Change-Shaping Levers

- Leadership: All leaders and managers play a crucial role in the ability of an organization to achieve its strategic and operational performance objectives through its people. For successful culture change to support the desired transformation they must consistently role model the desired new norms and behavior, and must also possess the right types of skills to manage all the people-related aspects of the initiative.
- Organizational Design and Structure: Levels of authority provide scope for behavioural changes by effectively defining what individuals are "allowed" to do, and accountabilities encourage these changes by conveying the message that employees will be held responsible for their actions. To promote effective change, authorities and accountabilities must be consistent and aligned with each other, and with the desired behaviours and norms. They are often reflected in the reporting structure. For example, a relatively flat, team-based structure is likely to be more

effective in promoting a culture in which employees work together on a project basis and make collective decisions, compared with a hierarchical structure in which important decisions are the responsibility of managers alone.
- Staffing and Deployment: Once the optimum reporting structure and roles and responsibilities within this have been defined, there will be a need to ensure that the roles are occupied by individuals who have the right skill sets and exhibit appropriate behaviours, and are therefore likely to interact with others in ways that will promote the desired new norms.
- Competency Development: Since the newly transformed organization will be expecting its employees and managers to behave in new ways or occupy new roles, and often to learn new skills in order to do so, a competency development strategy will be needed. This will often include formal training, as well as more informal competency development techniques such as mentoring, role modeling and opportunities for experiential learning.
- Performance Management: The performance-management system and performance criteria must be designed to effectively appraise and manage the performance of employees against the desired new behaviours. This is an important tool in cultural change since it provides the framework within which employees can be guided towards the "right" behaviours through a system involving performance planning and goal setting, regular appraisal and coaching to improve performance.
- Compensation, Rewards and Benefits: The compensation, rewards and benefits framework is similarly important in rewarding the desired behaviours or alternatively penalizing individuals who do not demonstrate this by withholding associated rewards and benefits. These systems need to be modified as necessary to ensure that they perform

- Communications: As a systemic change-shaping lever, communications are targeted mainly at groups of employees (e.g. in specific functional areas), and used to promote norms and behaviours that are expected to result in more sustained long-term culture change. Effective communications relating to strategic and operational goals, and what is required of groups in order to meet these, will be needed on a consistent, ongoing basis to ensure that the desired organizational culture is embedded and sustained.

To reiterate, therefore, in order to achieve successful transformation, there is a need not only for a strategic but also a holistic approach to change, which involves reviewing and re-aligning the organization's culture as well as its systemic change-shaping levers with the desired transformation goals.

In summary, we can thus describe effective organizational transformation as involving the transformation of the organization's people, processes, structure and culture to support the strategic objectives, within the context of the organization's core values and fundamental purpose. Understanding the importance of a strategic and holistic approach to transformation is an important first step in identifying the need to adequately prepare the organization to undergo the change initiative.

Another important step in this process is to understand the typical characteristics of transformation projects and how they differ from more traditional projects, giving rise to the need for new skill sets and mindsets. This is considered further in the following section.

CHARACTERISTICS OF NEW TRANSFORMATION PROJECTS

Traditionally, many projects typically involved a single sponsor, a clear consensus about the requirements, a co-located project team, a predictable environment and relatively low business risks. Most often, they were conducted to meet the functional rather than the strategic needs of the business.

In contrast, new types of transformation projects are highly complex. They frequently involve a number of different project sponsors and multiple stakeholder groups; may be implemented by geographically dispersed teams who are not directly employed by the organization, and are characterized by high levels of unpredictability and risk. They are also typically strategic in nature, with pressure to demonstrate high levels of Return on Investment (ROI) – and they often involve mission- critical changes for the organization.

These are "typical" features of prototype projects. There is of course in real life a wide continuum of projects in terms of budgets, complexity, the level of risk and so on, and every initiative has its own unique characteristics and challenges.

Nevertheless, there has been a strong movement towards the types of large and complex transformation projects described in the right-hand column of Table 1, which is dramatically changing the role and responsibilities of many Project Managers and the types of skills and expertise demanded of them.

Typical Traditional Project Characteristics	Typical New Project Characteristics
Operational or functional focus, often determined by short-term business needs	Strategic focus, guided by Fundamental Purpose and long-term business goals
Modest resource requirements	Large and resource-intensive
Usually a single project sponsor	May be multiple project sponsors with different priorities

THE NATURE AND CHARACTERISTICS OF TRANSFORMATION

Typical Traditional Project Characteristics	Typical New Project Characteristics
Mainly accountable to project sponsor	Greater direct accountability to senior organizational leaders and managers
Small number of stakeholders; general consensus about project goals and how to achieve them	Often multiple internal and external stakeholders with conflicting perspectives and interests
Relatively straightforward	Highly complex, with many inter-related challenges
Small, co-located project team	Large project team, often geographically and organizationally dispersed and culturally diverse
Relatively low, predictable and manageable risks	High level of potential risk from many sources
Familiar or predictable external environment	Highly unpredictable and volatile external environment
Focus on functional outcomes rather than ROI	Pressure to demonstrate value and ROI in short and longer term
Little or no requirement for project monitoring and evaluation	High requirement for monitoring and evaluation of project outcomes
Design, planning and implementation often based on relatively simple project management techniques	Requires a highly systematic and evidence-based approach to project design, planning and implementation

Table 1: Traditional and New Project Characteristics

As Table 1 highlights, new types of organizational projects are typically large, expensive and risky, an observation which is supported by research evidence.

A 2011 PMI Pulse of the Profession report noted, for instance, that organizations were "implementing increasingly large and more complex "high stakes" projects with an average budget of U.S.$4.4 million (Project Management Institute, 2011).

TRANSFORMATION PROJECT MANAGEMENT CHALLENGES

Since transformation projects are typically initiated through the organization's strategic planning process and are typically "high stakes" in nature, senior leaders and managers are taking a direct interest in these projects and their outcomes and often demanding more direct accountability to them from the Project Manager. There is an increased requirement to support project plans and budgets with evidence of "what works" and to monitor and report on project performance and value being generated.

An implication of all this is that Project Managers are now becoming much more directly involved in and contributing to the organization's core business planning process, something that was not typically required of them in the past. One author (Konstantopoulos, 2010) refers to the evolution of the "consultative project manager", who is "engaged in unearthing the business justification for the existence of the project, the recommended solutions that will satisfy the business needs and both determining and delivering the required executable actions needed to bring the solution to life".

The large scale and complex nature of many transformation projects also mean that they inevitably involve new and greater risks and challenges than more traditional projects. In the past, Project Managers had a high level of control over the project environment and there were relatively few sources of unpredictability. Project stakeholders, who were typically few in number, were generally supportive of the overall project goals and how to achieve them; any stakeholder conflicts or other challenges that arose could usually be managed fairly easily through mechanisms such as the project steering group.

THE NATURE AND CHARACTERISTICS OF TRANSFORMATION

In contrast, the project and stakeholder environment is very different for major organizational transformations. Since all parts of the organization, as well as external stakeholders such as business partners or supply chain participants, are often directly involved in the transformation, there is invariably a wide range of interests and perspectives that need to be reconciled and managed (Figure 5).

Figure 5: Project Stakeholders as per PMBOK®

Another challenge which many transformation managers face is also related to the complexity and multi-stakeholder nature of this type of project. To achieve the desired project outcomes, the Project Manager will generally need to rely on the direct inputs and contributions of many individuals and groups over whom they have little or no direct control or authority.

Moreover, depending on the characteristics and structure of the organization and its environment, the range of parties involved in the project may even span different countries and cultures. As Cleland & Ireland (2008) observe: "the challenges of stakeholder management seem to be exacerbated as a result of the varied political, cultural, and language differences faced by (international) projects."

This reduced control and influence of the Project Manager over stakeholders in major transformation projects also extends to the project team. As explained by Gillard (2009): "the project team itself is often large, and consists of a multi-faceted mix of multi-disciplinary, inter-organizational, geographically disbursed members, internally employed personnel, and outsourced or contract staff; the Project Manager must cope with tenuous lines of authority and power".

Overall, the Project Manager of a major organizational transformation will often operate in a very high risk, unpredictable environment over which they have relatively little direct control. Within this context, they have a high level of responsibility for delivering project outcomes that are crucial to overall business performance and the achievement of core business objectives.

In Chapter 4, we build on this discussion of the nature and characteristics of organizational transformation projects to highlight how, in this context, shortcomings in "traditional" project management are a major contributing factor to transformation project failures. We then set out our recommended Art and Science of Transformation® framework for project management. This addresses the shortcomings of traditional approaches by ensuring that the conventional "science" of project management skills are combined with the "art" skills that are necessary for managing the people and business aspects of transformation projects.

THE IMPORTANCE OF ART AND SCIENCE

Our discussion of the nature and characteristics of transformation projects in Chapter 3 highlighted the growing importance of people-related factors in project management, linked in particular to the complex, multi-stakeholder nature of such projects and the range of conflicting interests and perspectives involved. We also observed that Transformation Project Managers are often required to be closely involved in business and strategy development.

These initiatives, therefore, demand very different types of project management skills and attributes than in the past, with a shift away from primarily technical skills and towards the need for an understanding of the business and skillful stakeholder management.

WHY PROJECTS GO WRONG

An increasing body of published research-based evidence indicates that, when projects go wrong, this is not usually due to a lack of project management "science" – the formal tools and techniques involved in planning and executing an organizational transformation.

Instead, project failures can most often be attributed to a lack of attention to the people-related aspects or the "art" of transformation, such as communications, leadership and engaging employees in the transformation process. Conversely, the ability to apply "art" related skills effectively in project management has been shown to be associated with project success. For example:

- Business Executive respondents to an Economist Intelligence Unit survey about change management (2008) reported that the difficulties of winning over the hearts and minds of employees was the biggest barrier to a successful transformation, followed closely by securing the support of local managers. The same survey found that the factors most commonly cited as contributing to successful transformation were reported by respondents to be good leadership, planning and communication.
- The IBM Global Making Change Work Study (2008) identified "changing mindsets and attitudes" and "corporate culture", cited by 58% and 49% of respondents respectively, as the main barriers to effective organizational change.
- McKinsey & Co. examined the variables associated with successful organizational transformation projects, based on a global survey of executives, and found that the most important included good communications, effective employee engagement, the involvement of senior leaders and having clear change objectives.

This is not to suggest that the "science" of project management -- the formal tools and techniques used in estimating resource requirements, conducting a risk analysis, developing a budget and a project plan, and so on -- is unimportant.

On the contrary, studies have shown that the application of best-practice project management methods is one of the main factors associated with project success. KPMG New Zealand, for example, found that 90% of companies with a consistent track record of successful projects "always" or "often" used a project management methodology (KPMG NZ, 2013).

But using a methodological approach to project management is not enough, particularly in the case of large or complex projects, which typically involve a wide range of stakeholders, as well as "political" sensitivities or the need for an astute understanding of the business context. What is most important is to achieve the right balance of art and science for a successful transformation.

THE ART AND SCIENCE OF TRANSFORMATION® FRAMEWORK

Based on the empirical research evidence and our own hands-on experience of helping organizations of all types to successfully transform, Schroeder & Schroeder, Inc. developed the Art and Science of Transformation® framework to guide the identification and development of the right balance of skills for effective organizational transformation.

In this framework, we conceptualize the "science" of transformation as the formal project management techniques, methods and tools that are the focus of PMBOK® and other project management standards.

In contrast, we view the "art" of transformation as the more intangible or intuitive skills and attributes that are important in managing the people-related aspects of change and dealing with the strategic and business development aspects of transformation project management.

Some examples of "art" and "science" skills are shown in Table 2.

Project Management Art Skills Examples	Project Management Science Skills Examples
Effective leadership	Requirements-analysis techniques
Political acumen	Financial-planning and management methods

PREPARING FOR ORGANIZATIONAL TRANSFORMATION

Project Management Art Skills Examples	Project Management Science Skills Examples
Strategic Awareness	Time planning and management methods
Inter-personal communication skills	Work breakdown scheduling techniques
Team-building abilities	Project-performance measurement tools
Emotional intelligence	Risk-analysis techniques
Adaptability	Stakeholder-mapping and analysis techniques

Table 2: Examples of Art and Science Skills in Transformation Project Management

It is also useful to conceptualize the art and science of transformation in terms of mindsets, specifically the right combination of "right-brain" and "left-brain" thinking. Management of major transformation projects inevitably requires a mix of logical, rational and analytical left-brain thinking and creative, intuitive and holistic right-brain thinking, for example.

Figure 6 portrays the Art and Science balance that we believe to be crucial to effective transformation management.

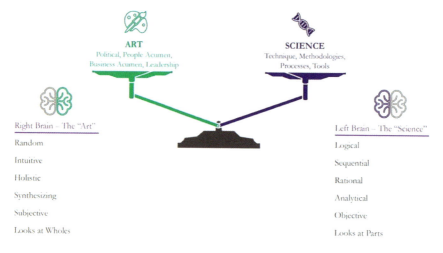

Figure 6: The Art and Science Balance

THE IMPORTANCE OF ART AND SCIENCE

Applying the right level of "art" to transformation project management will:

- Ensure that there is strong leadership which champions project interests and needs versus individual stakeholder interests;
- Ensure that the project and its goals are well aligned with business strategies;
- Ensure that different views on or interpretations of project objectives and goals are identified and reconciled;
- Ensure that project communication styles and methods are well-matched to the needs and characteristics of stakeholders and project team members;
- Ensure that agreement can be reached on how quality and risk are defined, taking account of different cultural or occupational perspectives;
- Increase motivation and commitment to the project; and
- Increase the probability of positive and sustainable outcomes.

Applying the right level of "science" to transformation project management will ensure that:

- All relevant stakeholders are identified and involved as necessary in the project;
- Detailed, accurate, comprehensive and achievable project plans are developed which mitigate the potential for later conflict or misunderstandings;
- A clear governance structure and project-related roles and responsibilities are all clearly defined;
- Appropriate use is made of communication tools and technology;
- Project risks are identified and managed;
- Adequate measures are developed and implemented to demonstrate project ROI; and
- All aspects of project execution are fully and accurately

documented in all relevant stakeholder environments, to enable effective monitoring, evaluation, scope and change control.

It's important to remember, however, that it is the combination of art and science skills – both within specific tasks and the transformation initiative overall – that is crucial for transformation success.

Here are a few examples of the ways that combinations of art and science skills are required in transformation projects:

- Identifying and specifying the project requirements and scope requires a good strategic understanding of the core business strategy and how this reflects the fundamental purpose and core values of the organization. It also requires the use of a systematic method of documenting and analyzing the needs and identifying the most cost-effective way of addressing these.
- Understanding the stakeholder-related project risks calls for emotional intelligence and sensitivity, as well as the use of systematic stakeholder mapping and analysis methods to ensure comprehensive identification and interpretation of these risks.
- Project finance and time-planning requires the ability to identify all types of quantitative and qualitative factors likely to influence the implementation, and to develop realistic plans and budgets which consider these, using best-practice planning techniques and tools.
- There will be a need to develop both quantitative and qualitative metrics and other indicators or project performance, to adequately capture progress towards organizational change outcomes. Qualitative indicators might be needed, for example, to measure increased engagement with customers or an improved organizational climate that helps motivate employees and increase their productivity.

THE IMPORTANCE OF ART AND SCIENCE

- A major, complex transformation will need to be managed systematically but not rigidly, allowing for the initiative to be adapted as necessary to a shift in the external environment or the changing demands of organizational leaders, while retaining a consistent focus on the ultimate objectives of the transformation.

Even in aspects of project management relating to people or culture, there is still a need for a "scientific" approach involving the use of formal or systematic techniques. For example, it is often important to be able to apply knowledge about governance methods and how to define decision-making responsibilities based on established best practice techniques.

Project Managers also need to be able to apply systematic methods for identifying the full range of project stakeholders, documenting their characteristics and developing stakeholder communications and management plans.

SHORTCOMINGS IN CONVENTIONAL PROJECT MANAGEMENT

Most Project Managers have a good knowledge and understanding of the "science" of project management, as set out in the Project Management Book of Knowledge or PMBOK® (PMI, 2004). This covers, for example, established methods and techniques for use in work scheduling, cost estimation and risk management.

But PMBOK® is really just a manual, focused primarily on the "typical" single and simple project situation. It sets out "what" should be done at each stage of the project, but provides relatively little guidance on "how" to deal with real-life project situations.

Unfortunately, project management training has not evolved in line with the changing nature of organizational projects. Project management training is still heavily focused on formal standards such as the Project Management Institute's PMBOK® Guide (PMI, 2008) and the Association for Project Management's Body of Knowledge

(APM, 2012), which take a similar approach to the "codification" of project management expertise, providing step-by-step guidance on how to manage a project. There are two major problems with this approach:

- The first is that real-life project situations, especially organizational transformation projects in today's business environment, are far too unpredictable and complex to be managed effectively in this way. Project Managers now need the types of skills and attributes that enable them to identify, understand and respond effectively and flexibly to challenges and issues faced on a daily basis.
- The second is that most project management standards view the project as a discrete, standalone entity that is relatively independent of its external environment. This again fails to reflect the reality of organizational transformation projects, which as discussed earlier, need to be conducted using a strategic and holistic approach.

Our intention is not to criticize the project management standards per se: they play an extremely valuable role in providing training and best-practice guidance on the technical, more quantitative aspects of project management. Indeed, later in this book we will use the PMBOK® project management processes as a framework when discussing the types of skills now needed for transformation project management.

But the standards are not only inadequate for today's project management; an overemphasis on these in project management training creates a new kind of project risk in the form of the Project Manager them self. This can be defined as the tendency for many Project Managers to operate "by the book", failing to understand what a successful transformation project consists of and how they can best achieve this by responding to the opportunities and challenges that arise in their own project situation. Also, the standards, while not neglecting the non-technical, people-related aspects of project management, do play these down in comparison to technical expertise.

Many other writers from around the world have long been questioning the relevance of project management standards and training to present-day project situations and suggesting ways in which they need to be improved. For example:

- Apfel et al. (2010) highlighted that project management standards focus on predictability rather than the expectation of change which is now an economic reality facing organizations (e.g. Apfel et al., 2010).
- Thomas & Mengel (2008) observed that formal project management training courses fail to prepare students for the real-life complexity of the project environment.
- Hällgren et al., (2012) argued that project management standards neglect the contextual and situational factors that influence project management, such as organizational procedures and the "trade-offs" that are so often necessary to get things done.
- Hodgson and Cimcil (2006) expressed concern that PMBOK® does not include moral or ethical considerations, giving rise to a misleading impression of being objective and straightforward (cited in Hällgren et al., 2012).
- Reich & Wee (2006) observed that the PMBOK® is focused on explicit knowledge, and highlight the importance of also finding ways of identifying and documenting the tacit knowledge that is gained within the organization through experience and understanding of the context (cited in Hällgren et al., 2012).
- Pappas (2005) observed that project manager training programs fail to address the ways in which projects have implications for and must be integrated with other areas of the business (cited in Egginton, 2012).
- Hartman (2008) argued that traditional project management training is focused on "left brain", logical thinking; this

- hinders the ability of Project Managers to identify and understand the bigger picture and the contextual factors influencing a project, especially those relating to human attitudes and behaviours (cited in Egginton, 2012).
- It has been argued that project management training has developed within a "hard" paradigm which focuses on quantitative techniques and deductive reasoning, rather than learning, participation and understanding of underlying social processes. The training of Project Managers frequently neglects the soft skills that must necessarily develop from experiential learning (cited in Egginton, 2012).
- Crawford et al (2006) argued that project management expertise should not be prescribed or codified, but should be focused on interpreting situations and developing the understanding of what to do and how to do it (cited in Egginton, 2012).

Why have project management standards and training become so badly misaligned with the current reality of the business environment? Perhaps it is at least partly because many organizations have not yet awoken to the considerable potential of the project management function as an organizational asset.

Even though there has been a documented large expansion in demand for project management professionals (Jugdey & Mathur, 2012; Zekic & Samarzija, 2012), there has been little demand from the business community to improve standards and training.

The Project Management Institute's Pulse of the Profession 2013, for example, reported that only around half of nearly 800 project management leaders and practitioners worldwide indicated that they fully understand the value of project management (PMI, 2013).

One of the objectives of this book is to demonstrate that the right kind of project management is probably one of the most important assets that any organization can have, and how to achieve this.

THE IMPORTANCE OF ART AND SCIENCE

DIFFERENT TYPES OF PROJECTS AND THE ART AND SCIENCE BALANCE

Not all projects require the same input or combination of art and science: the required skills and the balance of art and science will vary depending on factors such as project complexity, number and characteristics of stakeholders and perceived business risks.

One of the main challenges for organizations preparing for transformation is to identify the likely balance of art and science needed so that steps can be taken to ensure that the right people and expertise are in place.

In simple, functional projects with few stakeholders and low risks, the need for both art and science will generally be quite low. At the other extreme, a mission-critical program with multiple stakeholders will call for high inputs of both art and science.

Major transformation projects such as post-merger integrations or an enterprise-wide product or service launch often fall into this category, with all departmental heads or senior executives needing to be intimately involved in the initiative.

In between these extremes, there are a wide variety of organizational change projects and a need to judge in each case the relative importance of art and science and the specific skills and expertise needed for their effective management.

SUMMARY - THE ART AND SCIENCE OF TRANSFORMATION PROJECT MANAGEMENT

Transformation project management requires the right balance of:

- Art: the "soft", personal or intuitive skills needed for understanding and influencing people, or understanding the more intangible political or business-related aspects of the transformation

- Science: the application of specialized tools, methods and techniques in a systematic approach

Which can also be thought of as:

- "Right-brain" thinking: Holistic and qualitative
- "Left-brain" thinking: Analytical and logical

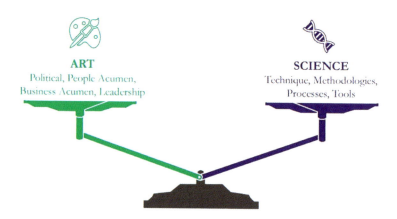

Based on the published research evidence as well as our own surveys and extensive hands-on experience of helping organizations to transform, we have attempted to tease out the specific reasons why a combination of art and science is needed for successful transformation management.

In doing so, we have identified two main factors that represent major risks to successful organizational transformation:

1. Deficiencies in project management
2. Deficiencies in project governance

This led to the conclusion that the Executive Sponsor, as well as the Project Manager of a transformation project, plays a crucial role in its success, because, as we shall discuss, the Executive Sponsor has important responsibilities with regard to both of these factors.

A critical success factor in transformation is, therefore, an effective

THE IMPORTANCE OF ART AND SCIENCE

partnership between the Project Manager and the Executive Sponsor of the transformation.

Additionally, the Executive Sponsor and the Project Manager must each be highly effective in performing their transformation responsibilities, and able to apply the right balance of art and science in their respective roles.

The following three Chapters explore these points in more detail, focusing in turn on the Executive Sponsor / Project Manager partnership, the role of the transformation Project Manager and the role of the Executive Sponsor.

THE EXECUTIVE SPONSOR / PROJECT MANAGER PARTNERSHIP

In Chapter 3 we described effective organizational transformation as involving the transformation of the organization's people, processes, structure and culture to support the strategic objectives, within the context of the organization's core values and fundamental purpose.

This demonstrates the extent to which a transformation project is not a stand-alone initiative but is inextricably integrated with and affected by many factors in the organizational environment, and largely explains the importance of the partnership between the Executive Sponsor and the Project Manager.

Many of these factors, as well as the multiple stakeholders involved in the transformation, fall outside the scope of the Project Manager's responsibility and control, yet these must be influenced in order to ensure the success of the transformation, a process in which the Executive Sponsor plays a central, facilitating role.

Both the Executive Sponsor and the transformation Project Manager are crucial to the success of a transformation project. What is of greatest importance is their ability to work together as a team, using their respective art and science skills in complementary ways to execute a successful transformation. In this chapter, we examine the nature of this relationship and the ways in which the respective roles of the Executive Sponsor and Project Manager complement one another in a successful transformation initiative.

The Project Management Body of Knowledge (PMI, 2013), defines a Project Sponsor somewhat narrowly, focusing on their role from conception of the project until the point at which the Project Manager takes on responsibility for its implementation, and just occasionally thereafter:

> "A sponsor is the person or group who provides resources and support for the project and is accountable for enabling success ... From initial conception through project closure, the sponsor promotes the project. This includes serving as spokesperson to higher levels of management to gather support throughout the organization and promoting the benefits the project brings. The sponsor leads the project through the initiating processes until formally authorized, and plays a significant role in the development of the initial scope and charter. For issues that are beyond the control of the Project Manager, the sponsor serves as an escalation path. The sponsor may also be involved in other important issues such as authorizing changes in scope, phase-end reviews, and go/no-go decisions when risks are particularly high." (PMI 2013, p. 32)

We believe that this description does not accurately reflect the full and important role of the Executive Sponsor and the partnership that must exist between them and the Project Manager for effective organizational transformation. This argument is supported by empirical evidence, for example:

In PMI's 2010 Government Program Management Study, 81% of program managers at U.S. government agencies said that strong support from at least one Executive-level sponsor had a high impact on project success.

A study of 1,000 project leaders from major corporations and smaller companies found that that 65% of Project Managers regularly experience problems due to the absence or ineffectiveness of project sponsors, including running over budget or behind schedule and failing to meet their objectives (Grenny, Maxfield & Shimberg, 2007).

GOALS, ROLES AND RESPONSIBILITIES

Understanding the important partnership between the Project Manager and the Executive Sponsor requires considering the different but inter-related types of goals that characterize a transformation project, and the ways in which the responsibility for meeting these is shared in the Project Manager / Executive Sponsor partnership.

A transformation project has two main types of goals:

- Operational goals, such as the targets for completing the project within a particular timescale and budget, and for delivering specific outputs to an agreed standard; and
- Strategic transformation goals, consisting of the intended organizational outcomes or ultimate impacts of the project.

The Executive Sponsor and the Project Manager are both responsible for ensuring that the initiative doesn't just achieve its operational goals but also its strategic transformation goals. However, they have different levels and types of responsibility in this respect.

It can be helpful to use the analogies of a Chief Executive Officer (CEO) and a Chief Operating Officer (COO) of a corporation in order to understand the roles and responsibilities of the Project Manager and Executive Sponsor with regard to these goals, and the ways they mesh together in a transformation initiative.

- The role of the Project Manager is similar to that of the COO of a corporation, who typically reports to the CEO.
    - The primary responsibility of the Project Manager is to ensure that the project achieves its

operational objectives, for which he or she is accountable to the Executive Sponsor as well as to the project Steering Committee.
- The Project Manager must also ensure that these operational goals are continually aligned with the strategic transformation objectives and that these ultimate goals can be achieved through the project's implementation.

- The role of the Executive Sponsor of the transformation corresponds with that of the CEO of a corporation:
    - The Executive Sponsor represents the interests of the organization as a whole in relation to the project and is in turn accountable to the organization for the achievement of the top-level strategic transformation goals.
    - The Project Manager cannot be held accountable for these since many of the actions necessary to achieve them will fall outside the sphere of their control and authority.
    - The other main role of the Executive Sponsor is to ensure that the project is appropriately managed and governed so that it is able to meet its operational as well as its strategic transformation objectives.

The partnership between the Project Manager and the Executive Sponsor is what enables them both to meet their own responsibilities and accountabilities with regard to the transformation.

Within this partnership, the Executive Sponsor supports the Project Manager by acting as the link between the project and the wider organization, ensuring that the necessary resources, as well as the inputs and contributions of various stakeholders, are secured.

He or she also provides senior-level input in terms of advice and guidance relating to the strategic context and core business objectives of the initiative, contributing detailed knowledge and understanding that the Project Manager cannot necessarily be expected to have.

Last but certainly not least, the Executive Sponsor is responsible for effective project governance, which involves establishing a strong governance structure and effective processes, to ensure that all stakeholders are adequately represented and involved in the initiative and that it is executed to high standards of ethics, transparency and accountability.

In contrast, as the COO of the transformation, so to speak, the Project Manager is instrumental in actually getting the things done that are necessary to achieve the operational and transformation objectives, facilitated as required by the higher-level actions taken by the Executive Sponsor, and in accordance with the governance standards and practices established by them.

The Project Manager will develop and execute the detailed project plan, including the project timeline, work breakdown schedule and budget, and lead and co-ordinate all the day-to-day activities of the transformation project team, an important and often challenging role which we discuss in more detail later in this chapter.

The main responsibilities of the Executive Sponsor and the Project Manager of an organizational transformation are set out in Table 3; this helps to show how these roles can be distinguished from one another and also how they are related and complementary.

Responsibility	Executive Sponsor	Project Manager
Strategy	■ Ensuring the project's strategic transformation objectives are aligned with core	■ Providing advice and support to assist the Executive Sponsor's strategic decision-making

Responsibility	Executive Sponsor	Project Manager
Governance	business goals - Providing strategic direction and guidance to Project Manager - Establishing a strong governance structure and effective processes - Ensuring that the project is executed to high standards of ethics, transparency and accountability - Ensuring that the interests of relevant stakeholders are represented in the initiative - Ensuring that stakeholders are kept adequately informed of project progress and consulted as necessary in decision-making	- Ensuring compliance with the defined governance requirements and processes, in project and team management
Leadership	- Acting as organizational champion and figurehead for the transformation initiative - Developing necessary linkages and relationships with senior	- Leading, guiding and supporting the project team in implementing the initiative - Leading and directing the organization as a whole in executing the transformation,

THE EXECUTIVE SPONSOR / PROJECT MANAGER PARTNERSHIP

Responsibility	Executive Sponsor	Project Manager
	stakeholders to facilitate project progress	including related communications, training and other activities
Management	<ul><li>Ensuring that the organizational environment is adequately prepared for the transformation, including the selection of an appropriate Project Manager</li><li>Ensuring that appropriate performance goals are identified and agreed with the Project Manager</li><li>Overseeing the monitoring of progress against performance targets and ensuring that problems or risks are addressed</li></ul>	<ul><li>Developing a detailed project plan and performance indicators</li><li>Estimating project resource requirements</li><li>Developing a detailed budget and work breakdown schedule</li><li>Appointing project team members and allocating tasks and responsibilities</li><li>Securing and co-ordinating inputs to the project from across the organization, within scope of own authority, or in collaboration with the Executive Sponsor</li><li>Managing day-to-day project work</li><li>Monitoring progress against performance targets and reporting to Executive Sponsor</li></ul>

Responsibility	Executive Sponsor	Project Manager
Accountability	■ Accountable to the organization as a whole, through the Steering Committee ■ Accountable for ensuring the project achieves its strategic transformation goals	■ Anticipating risks or obstacles to project and taking avoidance or mitigating actions ■ Accountable to Executive Sponsor and the Steering Committee ■ Accountable for ensuring the project achieves its operational goals so that it can achieve its transformation goals

Table 3: Responsibilities of the Executive Sponsor and Project Manager of a Transformation Initiative

ART AND SCIENCE IN THE PROJECT MANAGER / EXECUTIVE SPONSOR PARTNERSHIP

Based on the definition of responsibilities set out in Table 3, some key points can be made about the respective roles of the Executive Sponsor and the Project Manager of a transformation initiative, as follows.

The Executive Sponsor:

- Plays an important strategic role, linking the initiative with the organization's core business objectives and ensuring that it remains aligned with these;
- Is primarily responsible for the governance of the initiative, exercised largely through the project Steering Committee,

which represents the wider organization;
- Is the high-level champion and leader of the project;
- Ensures that the project is managed appropriately so that it can achieve its strategic transformation objectives as well as its operational objectives; and
- Is accountable to the organization as a whole, through the project Steering Committee

The Project Manager:

- Needs good strategic awareness and understanding, to manage the project effectively in ways that enable it to meet its strategic transformation objectives;
- Must comply with high standards of project governance;
- Leads and co-ordinates the project and all related activities on a day-to-day basis;
- Develops and executes the detailed project plan, including the project timeline, work breakdown schedule and budget;
- Appoints project team members and manages their day-to-day work;
- Monitors and reports on project progress against specified goals;
- Identifies and addresses risks to project performance; and
- Is accountable to the Executive Sponsor and the project Steering Committee

In carrying out their respective roles, the Executive Sponsor and the Project Manager need to possess both art and science skills in order to be able to work together successfully to bring about a successful transformation. As discussed earlier, the changing nature of projects and growing awareness of the reasons for project failure is increasing the need for Project Managers to have excellent art-related skills. At the same time, the growing complexity and scale of transformations require that Executive Sponsors understand the need for a methodical, systematic approach.

The need for an art- and science-based approach is equally relevant to the ways in which the Executive Sponsor and Project Manager work as a team: achieving an effective working relationship with the right mix of formal and informal communications requires both individuals to have good interpersonal skills and sensitivity to each other's preferred styles and methods of working.

An effective Executive Sponsor will be supportive and accessible but respectful of the role boundaries that exist between himself or herself and the Project Manager, and will avoid interfering in the details of project management or in the supervision of the project team while conveying approachability and understanding.

An effective Project Manager will be respectful of the demands on the Executive Sponsor's time, and will develop an astute understanding of when to consult with or involve them in project-related issues, and when to make independent decisions. They will also have the ability to communicate complex project issues in concise, straightforward ways, effectively conveying the key information that the Executive Sponsor needs for their own decision-making.

SUMMARY

An effective working relationship between the Project Manager and the Executive Sponsor of the transformation is essential because:

- The Executive Sponsor supports the Project Manager by acting as the link between the project and the wider organization, ensuring that the support and inputs of various stakeholders can be secured, especially when these fall outside the scope of the Project Manager's responsibility and control.
- The Project Manager and the Executive Sponsor also play different but complementary roles in relation to the inter-related objectives of the transformation:
    - The Executive Sponsor is accountable to the

organization for the achievement of the top-level strategic transformation goals.
- The Project Manager is accountable for the project's operational objectives, but must ensure that these continually promote the achievement of the strategic transformation objectives.

- The Executive Sponsor provides advice and guidance relating to the strategic context and core business objectives of the initiative, and supports the Project Manager by establishing a strong governance structure and effective governance processes for the transformation.

In the following two chapters, we examine the respective roles and responsibilities of the Project Manager and the Executive Sponsor in more detail and further explore the art- and science-related skills needed to perform these effectively, in order to bring about a successful organizational transformation.

TRANSFORMATION – THE ROLE OF THE PROJECT MANAGER

As discussed in Chapter 4, the types of skills and expertise required by Project Managers are changing dramatically. In the past, the main requirement was for "technical" knowledge of project management tools and techniques as set out in PMBOK®, Prince2 and other project management methodologies, and formally taught in project management training.

TRANSFORMATION PROJECT MANAGEMENT IS CHANGING

Some of the more significant changes in transformation project management include the following.

- Major and complex transformations involving all areas of the organization, multiple stakeholders and high levels of unpredictability have become commonplace in today's business environment
- As a result, the transformation Project Manager's role is more important than ever before, and central to the ability of an organization to meet its strategic goals.
- In this context, there has been a strong shift in emphasis

from technical project management expertise to business-related and interpersonal skills.

In the Art and Science of Transformation® framework, we define this technical expertise as the "science" of project management, which includes, for example, knowing how to develop a project budget, carry out a risk assessment, construct a work breakdown schedule, develop performance indicators and methods of monitoring progress against these etc., These are the focus of guidance and standards such as the Project Management Book of Knowledge (PMBOK®, 2013).

These days, however, the nature of organizational transformation projects has resulted in the need for an "art and science"-based approach to project management, in which business acumen and interpersonal skills are just as important as technical project management abilities. The "art" of project management consists of the personal attributes, or the types of skills that develop from experiential learning, that are especially important for managing the more subtle or people-related aspects of change. For example, these include interpersonal and communication skills, business acumen, political awareness, sound judgment and adaptability.

Table 4 illustrates some of the main ways that the application of art and science are important in transformation project management.

Importance of Science	Importance of Art
- Application of best-practice project management tools and methodologies, e.g. risk assessment and analysis; stakeholder analysis and management; performance measurement; time	- Ensuring that qualitative (people or culture-related) as well as quantitative factors are incorporated into project planning and management methods - Team building, interpersonal and communication skills for effective management of the

TRANSFORMATION – THE ROLE OF THE PROJECT MANAGER

Importance of Science	Importance of Art
planning; resource estimation; governance ■ Ensuring that an overall systematic and methodical approach is taken to managing the transformation initiative ■ Knowledge of legal and regulatory factors affecting the transformation, or ability to readily secure this.	project team and other project stakeholders ■ Ability to understand and utilize the impact of corporate culture on the organizational transformation ■ Recognition of the need for a holistic approach to transformation.

Table 4: Importance of Art and Science in Transformation Project Management

Table 5 shows some examples of the specific types of science and art skills important in transformation project management and their defining characteristics. These have been extracted from a total of 14 art skills and 14 science skills that were identified in a comprehensive review and analysis of project management literature.

To effectively manage a specific transformation initiative, the Project Manager will need to possess the right combination of art and science skills to meet the project requirements, or be able to draw on these as necessary within the project team to complement their own skill base.

It will also be important for them to possess an "art and science" mindset that incorporates both "right-brain" and "left-brain" thinking.

This helps to explain why a new type of Project Manager is needed for transformation management in today's business environment, not simply the addition of new project management skills.

Art Skills	Definition
Leadership	Engages, influences, inspires and guides others to meet goals; effectively represents team or organization to a range of stakeholders.
Business Acumen	Demonstrates an apparently instinctive understanding of the strategies and resources needed to achieve business success and growth, and how to implement these.
Strategic Awareness	Understands and consistently works towards the organizational strategy, mission and objectives.
Stakeholder Relations	Demonstrates awareness and understanding of internal and external stakeholder perspectives and addresses these effectively; is able to sustain stakeholder commitment.
People Acumen	Demonstrates an apparently instinctive ability to make sound judgments of the characters, traits and abilities of people, and their likely 'fit' to project team requirements.
Team building and Team Management	Develops and sustains co-operative working relationships; effectively delegates work and empowers others; is aware of team dynamics; effectively acknowledges and rewards individual and team contributions; fosters team spirit and pride.
Requirements Analysis and Project Scoping	Demonstrates and applies the principles, methods and abilities required to clarify and formalize project objectives and scope, including the development of a project charter, the specification of project deliverables and impact analysis.

TRANSFORMATION – THE ROLE OF THE PROJECT MANAGER

Art Skills	Definition
Financial Resource Planning and Management	Demonstrates and applies the principles, methods and abilities required to estimate financial resource requirements to achieve project goals, including a cost-benefit analysis, and to secure, manage and monitor these cost-effectively.
Project Time-Planning and Management	Demonstrates and applies the principles, methods and abilities required for estimating, planning and monitoring project activity time requirements and durations.
Project Governance	Demonstrates and applies the principles, methods and abilities required to establish and maintain an effective project governance structure.
Human Resource Planning and Management	Demonstrates and applies the principles, methods and abilities required for planning, securing and effectively managing human resources in order to achieve project objectives.
Stakeholder Management	Demonstrates and applies the principles, methods and abilities required for effectively identifying all project stakeholders, managing their expectations and securing their inputs in order to achieve project objectives.

Table 5: Example Art and Science Skills in Transformation Project Management

TRANSFORMATION MANAGEMENT TASKS, RESPONSIBILITIES AND SKILLS

In order to demonstrate the combined role of art and science in relation to the specific responsibilities and tasks of the Project Manager, we use a modified version of the PMBOK® stages of a project to define the key stages of a transformation project from an art and science of transformation perspective. Within this overall framework, we identify and discuss the types of art as well as science skills needed by the Project Manager.

PMBOK® (2008) identifies five key process groups as well as eight knowledge areas that cut across the process groups (Table 6). The mapping of knowledge areas and process groups as shown in this table can be regarded as the science of transformation management; with each of the tasks shown in the cells of the table drawing on best-practice tools and techniques.

Process Groups and Knowledge Areas	Tools and Techniques
Initiating Processes[1]	
Integration Management	Develop project charter
Stakeholder Management	Identify stakeholders
Planning Processes[2]	
Integration Management	Develop project management plan
Scope Management	Plan scope management; collect requirements; define scope; create Work Breakdown Structure (WBS)
Time Management	Plan schedule management; define and sequence activities; estimate activity resources and durations; develop schedule
Cost Management	Estimate costs and determine budget
Quality Management	Plan quality
Human Resource Management	Plan human resource management

TRANSFORMATION – THE ROLE OF THE PROJECT MANAGER

Process Groups and Knowledge Areas	Tools and Techniques
Communication Management	Plan communications management
Risk Management	Plan risk- management; identify risks; perform quantitative and qualitative risk analysis; plan risk responses
Procurement Management	Plan procurement management
Stakeholder Management	Plan stakeholder management
Executing Processes[3]	
Integration Management	Direct and manage project execution
Quality Management	Perform quality assurance
Human Resource Management	Acquire, develop and manage project team
Communication Management	Manage communications
Procurement Management	Conduct procurements
Stakeholder Management	Manage stakeholder engagement
Monitoring & Controlling Processes[4]	
Integration Management	Monitor and control project work; perform integrated change control
Scope Management	Validate scope; control scope
Time Management	Control schedule
Cost Management	Control costs
Quality Management	Perform quality control
Communication Management	Control communications
Risk Management	Control risks
Procurement Management	Control procurements
Stakeholder Management	Control stakeholder engagement

Process Groups and Knowledge Areas	Tools and Techniques
Closing Processes[5]	
Integration Management	Close project or phase
Procurement Management	Close procurements

Table 6. Mapping of project management process groups/knowledge areas (adapted from PMI, 2013)

[1] Performed to define a new project or a new phase of an existing project by obtaining authorization to start the project or phase.
[2] Required to establish the scope of the project, refine the objectives, and define the course of action required to attain the objectives that the project was undertaken to achieve.
[3] Performed to complete the work defined in the project management plan to satisfy the project specifications.
[4] Required to track, review, and regulate the progress and performance of the project; identify any areas in which changes to the plan are required, and initiate the corresponding changes.
[5] Performed to finalize all activities across all Process Groups to formally close the project or phase.

In Table 7 we build on this to describe the "art and science" of transformation project management in terms of specific examples of methods, tools, skills and attributes.

The science of effective transformation consists of the knowledge of and ability to use the types of tools and techniques shown in the second column of Table 7 and the art involves the types of skills and attributes shown in the third column of this table.

It can be seen that the "science" of transformation management is generally quite specific to particular knowledge areas and consists of the types of skills and expertise learned in formal training. In contrast, the important "art" skills in transformation management span many areas and largely reflect personal attributes and characteristics or the types of skills that develop from experiential learning.

PMBOK® Knowledge Areas	Science of Project Management Examples	Art of Project Management Examples
Integration management	<ul><li>Project management planning methods</li><li>Scheduling tools, e.g. Gantt charts, MS Project;</li><li>What-if scenario analysis</li><li>Impact Analysis</li></ul>	<ul><li>Business acumen</li><li>Strategic awareness</li><li>Sound judgment</li><li>Leadership</li><li>Team building/team management</li><li>Interpersonal skills</li></ul>
Scope management	<ul><li>Cost-Benefit analysis</li><li>Requirements analysis</li><li>Work breakdown scheduling techniques</li><li>Variance analysis</li></ul>	<ul><li>Political acumen</li><li>People acumen</li><li>Adaptability</li><li>Sound judgment</li><li>Intuition</li></ul>
Time management	<ul><li>Project Life Cycle Planning</li><li>Schedule Network Analysis, e.g. Critical Path Method, Critical Chain Scheduling)</li><li>Time-estimating techniques (Analogous, Parametric etc.)</li><li>Scheduling Tools</li></ul>	<ul><li>Holistic focus</li><li>Sound judgment</li><li>Interpersonal skills</li><li>Communication skills</li></ul>

PMBOK® Knowledge Areas	Science of Project Management Examples	Art of Project Management Examples
Cost management	<ul><li>Cost estimation techniques</li><li>Reserve analysis</li><li>Earned Value Management</li><li>Variance Analysis</li><li>Cost-forecasting Techniques</li><li>Cost-Benefit Analysis</li></ul>	<ul><li>Business acumen</li><li>Focus on results</li><li>Sound judgment</li><li>Holistic focus</li></ul>
Quality management	<ul><li>Cost of Quality techniques</li><li>Metrics design</li><li>Benchmarking</li><li>Quality audits and inspections</li><li>Project performance reviews</li><li>Program Evaluation and Review Technique</li></ul>	<ul><li>Focus on results</li><li>Sound judgement</li><li>Holistic focus</li><li>Qualitative perspective</li></ul>
Human Resource management	<ul><li>Roles and responsibilities matrices</li><li>Organizational structure planning</li><li>Human resource planning methods</li><li>Skills evaluation tools and techniques</li></ul>	<ul><li>People acumen</li><li>Leadership</li><li>Team building/ management skills</li><li>Emotional intelligence</li><li>Relationship-building skills</li><li>Ability to evaluate qualitative skills</li></ul>

TRANSFORMATION – THE ROLE OF THE PROJECT MANAGER

PMBOK® Knowledge Areas	Science of Project Management Examples	Art of Project Management Examples
Communication management	<ul><li>Communications planning</li><li>Electronic project management tools, e.g. scheduling tools, virtual office support software, collaborative work-management tools.</li><li>Performance-reporting tools (e.g. Balanced Scorecards)</li></ul>	<ul><li>Communication skills</li><li>People acumen</li><li>Sound judgement</li><li>Focus on results</li><li>Strategic awareness</li><li>Holistic focus</li></ul>
Risk management	<ul><li>SWOT analysis</li><li>Assumptions analysis</li><li>Risk probability and impact assessment</li><li>Risk data quality assessment</li><li>Risk-response strategy planning</li><li>Variance and trend analysis</li><li>Critical Path analysis</li><li>Risk audits</li><li>Risk-analysis software (e.g. Monte Carlo)</li></ul>	<ul><li>Business acumen</li><li>Political acumen</li><li>Strategic awareness</li><li>Sound judgment</li><li>Focus on results</li><li>Adaptability</li><li>Intuitiveness</li><li>Emotional intelligence</li><li>Holistic focus</li></ul>
Procurement management	<ul><li>Make-or-buy analysis</li><li>Vendor-bid</li></ul>	<ul><li>Business acumen</li><li>Focus on results</li><li>Sound judgment</li></ul>

PMBOK® Knowledge Areas	Science of Project Management Examples	Art of Project Management Examples
	Analysis - Contract management - Specialist knowledge of contract types - Procurement performance reviews - Knowledge of relevant procurement-related laws and regulations	- People acumen - Adaptability
Stakeholder Management	- Governance theory and methods - Stakeholder-mapping and analysis techniques	- Strategic awareness - Political acumen - People acumen - Interpersonal skills - Emotional intelligence - Intuition - Interpersonal skills - Holistic focus

Table 7: The Science and Art of Transformation Project Management, by PMBOK® Knowledge Areas

To a large extent, therefore, the identified "art" skills and attributes indicate the "type" of Project Manager needed for effective organizational transformation, both in terms of personality and experience. They also naturally overlap since they reflect the type of holistic approach to transformation management (based on both right-brain and left-brain thinking) that has become increasingly important in today's business environment, as discussed earlier.

Let's examine some of these art skills and their importance in transformation project management in a bit more detail. Due to the overlapping nature of these skills, we can identify five important skill "clusters" in the art of transformation project management.

Cluster 1: Business Acumen / Strategic Awareness:	■ These types of skills are important to ensure that the Project Manager easily grasps the wider business relevance of the project and understands how it is to contribute to the achievement of the top-level transformation goals, within the context of the organizational purpose and core values.
	■ They help to ensure that the Project Manager steers the transformation initiative effectively towards the achievement of its operational and transformation goals, modifying the scope and activities as necessary to reflect shifts in the wider environment or the priorities of organizational leaders, in order to deliver the desired outcomes.
	■ Strategic awareness and business acumen also enable the Project Manager to interact and communicate effectively with a range of organizational stakeholders, including the top-level transformation team and the Executive Sponsor.

- Business acumen provides the Project Manager with an almost instinctive understanding of the strategic transformation objectives and operational goals of the project, the strategies and resources needed to achieve these, and how best to implement them.

- This skill cluster also provides the Project Manager with the ability to understand the inter-relationships and interdependencies between different areas of the business and the relevance of these to the project.

- Project Managers with good business acumen will be mindful of the financial and business implications of project developments and decision-making, and will attempt to maximize their business value while minimizing project risks.

Cluster 2: Leadership / Team Building / Relationship Building

- Along with the Executive Sponsor, the Project Manager has a primary responsibility for driving the project and securing the efforts of others in order to achieve the operational and transformation goals.

- Leadership, teambuilding and relationship-building skills are essential in order to engage, influence, inspire and guide all project stakeholders and participants.

TRANSFORMATION – THE ROLE OF THE PROJECT MANAGER

- An important aspect of this skill cluster is the ability to quickly develop trust-based relationships with stakeholders and to create a project environment in which these are readily formed, e.g. in the project implementation team and the high-level transformation team.

- Doing so draws on a range of interpersonal and communication skills, as well as the intuitive ability to understand people and their interests and concerns and to demonstrate this effectively.

- It also requires the ability to identify and effectively resolve or manage conflicts, while developing a sense of shared team identity and goals.

- Another important aspect of this skills cluster is being able to effectively articulate and communicate the project vision and mission and to inspire and motivate others to work towards these.

- Effective leadership and team building also involve the ability to confidently delegate work and empower others, while maintaining sufficient high-level oversight of project activities and influencing factors.

Cluster 3: People Acumen / Political Acumen

- Political acumen and people acumen involve the almost intuitive ability to discern and understand the perspectives and interests of individuals

- and groups, as well as their personal traits and abilities.
- This includes being able to understand and navigate the power structures that often exist within organizations in order to secure the necessary contributions to the transformation and overcome people-related barriers to project progress.
- It also involves understanding that leaders have both "corporate agendas" and "personal agendas" and how to manage these in the best interests of the overall organization and the transformation goals.
- A Project Manager with good people acumen and political acumen will have an intuitive awareness of how to interact and communicate with others in order to achieve positive outcomes, and an instinctive ability to anticipate or recognize people-related problems and project risks and to understand how best to resolve these.
- They will also be sensitive to social and cultural differences and to differences in seniority, and will tailor project communications accordingly.

Cluster 4: Intuition / Sound Judgment / Emotional Intelligence

- Effective transformation Project Managers will draw on right-brain as well as left-brain thinking, using their intuition, emotional intelligence and

- sound judgment to complement hard evidence in project decision-making.

- Intuition refers to the ability to instinctively grasp a situation or issue and identify the best solution or course of action.

- This skill cluster provides an attuned, holistic awareness of the overall state of progress on a project, which is greater than the combined information available on its component parts, and represents and is an important aspect of a balanced, whole-brain (art- and science-based) approach.

- Often, an intuitive feeling that something is right or wrong is likely to be based on previous experiences or accumulated knowledge; Project Managers who are skilled in this area will be able to identify the source of this feeling in order to judge whether it is accurate in the current project context and to justify decisions made.

Cluster 5: Flexibility / Adaptability / Agility

- Transformation Project Managers need a high degree of flexibility, adaptability and agility in order to operate in the fast-changing, highly volatile business environment and continually steer projects towards their transformation goals, modifying the project scope as necessary to reflect changing circumstances.

- A flexible approach to transformation project management also involves selecting project management tools and approaches according to the needs of the project rather than personal preference and adapting one's own management and leadership style to the characteristics of the project and its stakeholders.

This section sets out the types of skills required for effective transformation project management in today's environment, using a framework which combines our Art and Science of Transformation® approach with the PMBOK® map of project management processes and knowledge areas. This has highlighted the importance of a new type of Project Manager, who not only possesses the knowledge and the ability to apply best-practice tools and techniques (the science) but also exhibits personal traits and skills derived from experiential learning that are crucial for the management of large, complex transformation projects with multiple stakeholders.

MANAGEMENT OF THE HIGH-PERFORMANCE TRANSFORMATION PROJECT TEAM

A major transformation project will also involve another important entity that is crucial for its success and which has a significant impact on the skill requirements and responsibilities of the Project Manager: the transformation project team.

Establishing a project team or teams that collectively provide the necessary functional and specialist knowledge, skills and expertise is essential to the success of a transformation initiative. A high-performance team working towards the operational and transformation objectives is a powerful driving force in the success of the project.

TRANSFORMATION – THE ROLE OF THE PROJECT MANAGER

A transformation project team will generally be drawn from different functional or specialist areas of an organization, and often from multiple organizations, for example when the project involves business partners or supply chain participants. Independent contractors or consultants may also be included, when commissioned to provide technical or specialist expertise.

Managing the work of the transformation project team(s) is central to the role of the transformation Project Manager and is typically much more challenging than more conventional project team management due to the complexity, high-stakes nature and other characteristics of organizational transformation projects.

For example, specific challenges may include:

- Motivating and leading a newly formed team to perform quickly and deliver results within a short timescale.
- Managing and coordinating the work of multiple project teams with different functional roles, while maintaining a focus on the "big picture" and overall objectives of the project.
- Using interpersonal skills to influence the behaviours of people over which the Project Manager has no direct authority.
- Challenges relating to the management of a geographically dispersed or culturally diverse team.

Some of the typical features of transformation project teams and their implications for project management are as follows

Pressure to perform quickly:	- The team members are likely to consist of individuals from diverse areas or different organizations, who may not have worked together before and may not know one another personally.

- Typically, in a major, high-stakes organizational transformation project, they will be required to get up to speed and make concrete progress against the implementation plan relatively quickly, in a high-risk environment where mistakes will be very costly for the organization.

- In this context, there is little time for the transformation team to proceed through the normal stages of group formation, defined by Tuckman (2001) as "forming, storming, norming, performing, and adjourning". These usual stages involve getting to know one another, overcoming differences and gradually developing a sense of shared identity which facilitates high levels of performance towards the achievement of group goals.

- In a major organizational transformation, it will be crucial for the team to reach the high level "performing stage" as quickly as possible, largely skipping the preceding stages. To achieve this, the Project Manager will need to actively drive and influence the process of group formation and performance, drawing on crucial stakeholder management and interpersonal skills to reconcile team differences, motivate and inspire the team towards shared project goals

TRANSFORMATION – THE ROLE OF THE PROJECT MANAGER

	and ensure that they are continually delivering progress against the implementation plan.
Multiple team structure:	▪ The transformation project team will in practice often consist of a number of separate teams, with respective responsibilities for implementing different aspects of the transformation. For example, separate teams may be responsible for technical change, restructuring, human resource systems change, cultural transformation, and so on.
	▪ As a result, there will be many interdependencies between different project tasks and activities that need to be managed. The Project Manager will need to ensure that the work of the respective teams is properly integrated so that the project goals can be achieved efficiently and cost-effectively without unnecessary hindrances or delays.
	▪ Addressing this challenge will require the expert use of advanced project planning and scheduling tools and techniques and often the use of collaborative work tools such as SharePoint, Workshare and Basecamp. But the ability to build an effective transformation project team which works in a coordinated way will also require excellent leadership and

- communication skills, to ensure that all team members work in harmony towards the operational and transformation goals of the initiative.

- It will often be helpful to establish a coordinating group consisting of team leaders. This group will represent an important co-ordination and control mechanism for the project, helping to reduce the risk of inter-team conflict by promoting a sense of shared identity through collaborative project planning and issue resolution.

- The Project Manager also needs to be able to step back and focus on the "big picture" of the transformation, identifying the linkages and inter-dependencies and managing these effectively, while the individual project team leaders address the detailed day to day aspects of implementation in their own areas. This requires the ability to empower others and to delegate effectively while maintaining oversight of team performance and outcomes and intervening when necessary to keep the project on track to meet its operational and performance goals.

Different lines of authority:

- A transformation project team will usually be drawn from across the organization or from multiple stakeholder organizations, representing

- the range of functional or specialist areas necessary to successfully implement the project.

- One major implication is that the transformation Project Manager may have little or no direct authority over team leaders or team members. These individuals will often report to different line managers and will have competing demands on their time.

- Depending on the nature of the transformation and the need for direct senior-level input, project team leaders may even be higher in the organizational structure than the Project Manager.

- When the transformation Project Manager is required to secure and manage the contributions or activities of people over which they have no direct authority, there is a need to rely heavily on good interpersonal and communication skills, especially the ability to motivate and engage others, as well as good negotiation and persuasion skills.

- The Project Manager will also need to be able to understand the perspectives and interests of different stakeholder groups represented in the project team. This will enable them to relate to team members in the right "language" to help secure their commitment to the overall goals of the transformation and their willingness to work towards these.

Cultural and interdisciplinary diversity:

- Major transformations will often involve a project team that includes individuals from different national, functional or professional cultures.

- This diverse group may have differing perspectives on and interpretations of project goals and how best to achieve them. The role of the Project Manager will be to identify any potential project risks arising from these, and ensure that important differences are addressed and reconciled. In particular, there is a need to ensure that a consensus exists on how quality and risk should be defined in the project context.

- The Project Manager will also need to ensure that project communication styles and methods are well matched to stakeholders' national cultures and/or their functional and professional backgrounds, so as to secure their commitment to the transformation as well as a good understanding of the requirements.

- When multi-country project teams are involved, there are unique challenges relating to understanding different cultural norms and values and achieving the right "tone" and content of communications, so as not to cause misunderstanding or offense. In some cultures, the very notion of team-working is quite alien, and there may, therefore, be a need to ensure that team members understand their team-related roles and responsibilities.

Geographically dispersed:

- A complex transformation will often require a transformation project team that is dispersed across different locations, either on multiple sites of the same organization or in separate organizations (for example when supply chain participants or business partners are involved).

- This presents particular logistical and communication challenges, as well as exacerbating the difficulties of creating a shared team identity.

- The Project Manager will need to rely heavily on electronic communication methods and "virtual" meetings, for example using Skype or similar video-conferencing tools. With a lack of informal face-to-face communications, it will be essential to make optimum use of team meetings, with detailed advanced planning of the agenda and goals, and clear, accurate follow-up communications that confirm agreed actions and responsibilities.

- The Project Manager should also implement and encourage the use of

- Managing team members from a distance presents particular challenges for the transformation Project Manager: it will be more difficult to maintain a high level of awareness about project progress in different parts of the country or the world and to identify and address any emerging risks. Establishing a system of frequent progress reports will help overcome these difficulties, but developing trust-based working relationships is just as important, as these will help ensure that team members can be relied on to meet their responsibilities and will help promote transparency and good communications.

collaborative work and knowledge management tools such as SharePoint, Workshare and Basecamp.

TRANSFORMATION PROJECT MANAGEMENT – CASE STUDY

In Canada, as in other countries, complex, collaborative transformation projects are becoming increasingly common in both the private and the public sector. This is largely a result of the various drivers of change discussed earlier in the book: competitive pressures, regulatory requirements, technological advances and so on.

The importance of an art and science approach to transformation project management in this context can be illustrated by an example from Schroeder & Schroeder, Inc.'s consulting experience.

We were commissioned by a relatively new non-profit, shared services organization, with approximately 4,000 clients. The organization was facing a considerable expansion in its

TRANSFORMATION – THE ROLE OF THE PROJECT MANAGER

responsibilities and needed to implement a new enterprise information system to support its growing business. Its existing data systems were managed by external services providers, a situation which resulted in inefficiencies and considerable business risks, including a lack of access to the high-quality data needed to manage the expanding business. The organization was also required to meet increasing requirements for compliance reporting to the government.

Our experiences of conducting this project demonstrated the importance of achieving a good balance of art and science in project management and in particular, the ways in which art skills were crucial for the successful completion of a project that, on the surface, appeared to require mainly technical or "science" skills.

This project involved major challenges over and above the technical aspects of system development. In order to bring about a successful project outcome, we needed to understand and address a range of organizational and people-related issues that were unique to the organization and its situation.

The key characteristics of this complex and high-risk transformation project, which presented a range of challenges for the project team, included:

- Multiple stakeholders – client, provincial government, industry representatives, municipalities, data suppliers, external service providers.
- A newly formed organization with under-developed strategic awareness and few formalized business processes.
- A need to integrate disparate information systems that were previously outsourced to external service providers.
- A high profile project in a politically sensitive area.
- A project team including many stakeholders: client representatives, external service provider representatives, newly recruited staff, and project business analysts and IT specialist

These characteristics, combined with the objectives of the project and a tight timescale for delivery, meant that the project involved a number of major challenges, including the need to:

- Secure collaborative efforts between the project team, the client, the former outsourcers, and the IT service organization, who were based in many in different locations and comprised very different types of organizations.
- Understand and manage disparate stakeholder expectations of and perspectives on the project – including the prospect of no co-operation from service providers who have little to gain from its successful implementation.
- Maintain adequate communications with and input from stakeholders and project team members outside the client organization, including those with little direct interest in the outcomes.
- Clarify business requirements with relatively little guidance from the client, since there was no precedent for a project of this type in the relatively new organization.
- Deliver the project to a very tight timeline to meet regulatory requirements.
- Establish a project team with suitable expertise, including the procurement of an external IT service provider.

The complexities and sensitivities involved in this project called for a high input of both art and science. Below are examples of some situations that arose on the project and their associated risks and shows how both art and science were instrumental in overcoming the challenges and contributing to a successful outcome for the project.

As shown, the types of art skills that were especially beneficial to this project included leadership, interpersonal communication skills, strategic awareness and sensitivity. Equally important science skills included the ability to conduct best-practice requirements analysis and project planning, and to apply problem-solving and analytical expertise to the project challenges and develop the project solution.

TRANSFORMATION – THE ROLE OF THE PROJECT MANAGER

PROJECT SITUATION 1:

Key stakeholders (service providers) initially failed to acknowledge the need for or benefits of the project.

Risk involved:	■ Lack of commitment of key stakeholders to project goals would jeopardize project implementation
How Science Helped:	■ Problem-solving and analysis skills ensured that the reasons for project resistance were understood and overcome.
How Art Helped:	■ Sensitivity to the concerns and perspectives of a range of stakeholders helped reduce conflict and maximize their commitment and cooperation.
	■ Strategic awareness ensured that the project was clearly aligned with organizational goals, helping to secure stakeholder commitment.

PROJECT SITUATION 2:

Difficulties were encountered in obtaining necessary input from external stakeholders (former service providers).

Risk involved:	■ System could be designed on the basis of incomplete or inaccurate information and not meet business needs.

How Science Helped:	■ Good expertise in requirements analysis and problem-solving skills enabled the project team to clearly define information requirements, reducing the workload and effort required by stakeholders.
	■ Resourcefulness was important in identifying alternative strategies or sources.
How Art Helped:	■ Good interpersonal skills were crucial in developing and maintaining effective working relationships with external stakeholders.
	■ A strong focus on results helped ensure perseverance when confronted with difficulties.

PROJECT SITUATION 3:

Project team was placed under pressure by a tight project deadline resulting from external requirements

Risk involved:	■ Potential failure to meet project deadline
	■ Potential for project errors
	■ Potential for conflict within project team.

TRANSFORMATION – THE ROLE OF THE PROJECT MANAGER

How Science Helped:	■	Detailed project planning ensured that the goals were achievable and enabled continuous progress monitoring against plans, so that necessary adjustments could be made.
	■	Strong leadership was essential in driving the project to a successful outcome
How Art Helped:	■	Effective team building resulted in shared commitment to meeting project goals despite difficulties
	■	High level of verbal communication between the Project Manager and team members enabled risks to be quickly identified and addressed.

Despite the significant challenges we faced on this project, the application of the right balance of art and science enabled us to successfully meet the objectives of the project. As a result,

the client now holds all its business data internally on a single integrated system and has the ability to generate live data and automated reports for the purpose of program reporting and business intelligence purposes. By developing a clear understanding of the client's business based on an art and science approach we were also able to add value by helping the organization develop a clear business vision for the future, and a roadmap for achieving it.

PREPARING FOR ORGANIZATIONAL TRANSFORMATION

This section has identified the types of skills required for effective transformation project management in today's environment, using a framework which combines our Art and Science of Transformation® approach with the PMBOK® map of project management processes and knowledge areas.

This has highlighted the importance of a new type of Project Manager, who not only possesses the knowledge and the ability to apply best-practice tools and techniques (the science) but also exhibits personal traits and skills derived from experiential learning that are crucial for the management of large, complex transformation projects with multiple stakeholders.

In Chapter 7 we examine the responsibilities of the other key player in the transformation management process, the Executive Sponsor, and identify the main types of art and science skills required in this role.

TRANSFORMATION – THE ROLE OF THE EXECUTIVE SPONSOR

> As projects become more complex and high risk, strong project governance is especially important, as well as the ability to apply the right balance of art and science skills in transformation project management. This has elevated the role of the Executive Sponsor, who is responsible for ensuring that these are in place. Additionally, the Executive Sponsor plays an important role in connecting the transformation project with the wider organization and ensuring that it achieves the intended strategic objectives.

THE IMPORTANCE OF THE EXECUTIVE SPONSOR

The association between effective executive sponsorship and project success is well supported by the published research evidence.

In PMI's 2010 Government Program Management Study, 81% of program managers at U.S. government agencies said that strong support from at least one Executive-level sponsor had a high impact on project success.

Unfortunately, although effective executive sponsorship is known to be associated with project success, there is also evidence that few companies apply this in practice to their organizational transformation projects. Shortcomings in the performance of the Executive Sponsor's role, especially with regard to project governance, often represent the weak link that can lead to project failure. For example:

- Research with more than 1,000 project leaders in Fortune 500 multinationals as well as smaller companies revealed that 65% of Project Managers had regularly experienced problems due to the absence or ineffectiveness of project sponsors, and more than three-quarters of projects with these sponsorship problems ran over budget, behind schedule and failed to meet their objectives. Eleven percent, it was estimated, ran over budget by more than a million dollars (Grenny, Maxfield & Shimberg, 2007).
- The KPMG New Zealand Project Management Survey (2010) found that problems arise in projects when there is a lack of executive sponsorship and management buy-in (in PMI). This study revealed that an effective project sponsor was often lacking in 68% of the companies surveyed (KPMG, 2010).
- In case study research which investigated more than 20 failed or failing projects, it was discovered that each one had lacked an effective project sponsor (Thomsett International, cited in Patton & Shechet, 2007).

Despite these statistics, relatively little research has been conducted into the role of the Executive Sponsor, in contrast with the Project Manager's role. As a result, there is often confusion and uncertainty about the Executive Sponsor's responsibilities (Anderson, 2012; Crawford & Brett, 2001; Kloppenberg et al., 2009).

This has made it difficult to identify good practice in Executive Sponsorship that can be widely adopted to improve transformation project performance (Labuschagne et al., 2006).

TRANSFORMATION – THE ROLE OF THE EXECUTIVE SPONSOR

Within our Art and Science of Transformation® approach, we identify three major roles of the Executive Sponsor which are especially important in contributing to a successful organizational transformation:

- Preparing the organization for an "art and science"-based transformation
- Project governance
- Achieving the strategic transformation objectives

In the following sections, we discuss these aspects of the Executive Sponsor's role in more detail, examining what is involved in successfully performing each of these roles and identifying the types of skills and expertise required in each case.

ORGANIZATIONAL READINESS FOR AN "ART- AND SCIENCE"-BASED TRANSFORMATION

The first important role of the Executive Sponsor, once a decision has been taken to go ahead with a transformation initiative, is to ensure that the organization is adequately prepared for an art and science-based transformation that will deliver sustained business value. This role has two main components:

- Selecting the Project Manager. This involves determining the types and balance of art and science skills needed for the transformation project and overseeing the Project Manager selection process to ensure the right person for the job is appointed.
- Assessing organizational change-readiness. This is important so that potential barriers to change can be addressed, and to help ensure that the intended transformation objectives can actually be achieved.

There is a need at this stage to ensure that there is a good understanding in the organization of the types of art and science skills that are necessary for successful transformation project management, and to take the necessary measures to ensure that these are in place. This role also involves ensuring that the existing organizational culture and systems are not likely to hinder a successful transformation and take steps to identify any necessary change.

Table 9 summarizes the ways in which both art and science are needed in the Executive Sponsor role.

Importance of Science	Importance of Art
<ul><li>Understanding the importance of a systematic approach to transformation management</li><li>Having an adequate knowledge of project management tools and methodologies, to support and advise the Project Manager in their work</li><li>Knowledge of and ability to implement best-practice project governance structures and processes</li></ul>	<ul><li>Strong leadership skills, especially the ability to inspire and motivate others to engage with and contribute to the transformation</li><li>Excellent interpersonal and communication skills for interaction with a range of internal and external stakeholders at different levels</li><li>Good negotiating and persuasion skills to secure resources and support for the project</li><li>Political and business acumen to identify all the relevant risks and opportunities relating to the project.</li></ul>

Table 9: Importance of Art and Science in the Executive Sponsor Role

TRANSFORMATION – THE ROLE OF THE EXECUTIVE SPONSOR

SELECTION OF THE PROJECT MANAGER

Before a transformation project is implemented, it is crucial to investigate whether the organization has the right combination of art and science project management skills in place, and take the necessary measures to address any gaps, through recruitment, training, or contracting out of the project management function.

Most major or complex transformation projects will require high levels of both art and science to ensure their success, but the specific balance of art and science required will vary among projects. This needs to be taken into account when making initial important decisions such as whether to recruit a new Project Manager, contract out project management or appoint someone from within the organization to manage the project and should be used to form the selection criteria.

For any organizational transformation to succeed, it will, therefore, be important to achieve the right balance of art and science, in terms of the skills and abilities of the Project Manager and the project team. Since most people have a tendency to be either mainly "right-brain" or "left-brain" thinkers, there is a need to ensure that the project team as a whole has a good balance of both types of individual, who can communicate and work well together despite their different approaches.

Typical transformation projects require Project Managers who have, for example, knowledge of the company and its industry, good business acumen, people management skills, and the emotional intelligence so often necessary for really understanding the range of influences on a project and determining how to respond to these.

These "softer", people-focused skills often underpin the ability to successfully implement project management tools and techniques. For example, the ability to define the scope and objectives of a project is not enough – a Project Manager must also be able to communicate these effectively to all stakeholders in a way that secures their commitment to the project.

Similarly, Project Managers who are skilled in producing Gantt Charts also need the intuitive ability to identify all kinds of risks to timely project completion.

A project matrix such as that shown in Figure 6 can be used to help determine the balance of art and science project management skills needed for the transformation project, based on the relative complexity of the project.

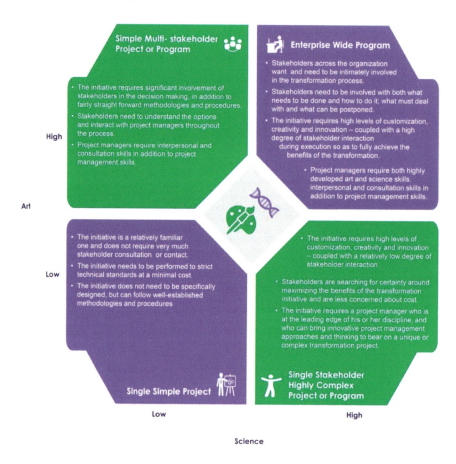

Figure 6: *Types of Project and the Need for Art and Science*

Unfortunately, just as project management standards and training have not yet evolved to reflect the demands of the new business environment, neither have project management assessment methods, which also closely reflect the formal standards.

This means that, when recruiting and selecting Project Managers, organizations tend to rely heavily on written tests or structured questionnaires which have been developed primary to test the "science" of project management, but are much less well suited to an evaluation of a Project Manager's "art" expertise.

Evaluating project management art skills, which are often only demonstrated through real-life experience rather than formal qualifications, requires the use of more qualitative methods such as in-depth interviewing, detailed review of resumes or performance reports or a 360-degree assessment process.

These types of methods not only provide information on the "soft" skills of Project Managers but on whether they have the right type of mindset to manage the transformation initiative using an art and science-based approach.

An organization's Human Resource management function cannot be expected to achieve this type of assessment independently. This is because selecting the most appropriate Project Manager requires an astute understanding of the balance of art and science skills needed to successfully manage the project, which in turn requires an understanding and awareness of the wider business context, organizational politics, stakeholder interests and possible conflicts of interest and so on.

The Executive Sponsor should, therefore, work closely with the HR department to ensure they understand the specific project management requirements for the initiative and develop recruitment or selection systems designed to explore and assess both art and science skills.

If gaps in the required art and science skills are identified, either at the individual or organizational level, the process of filling these must be initiated.

Depending on the urgency of the transformation initiative and the importance to the project of the required skills that are missing or in short supply, this might be achieved by contracting out the management of the project; by recruiting a new Project Manager, or by training and developing existing staff.

ORGANIZATIONAL CHANGE READINESS

Another important role of the Executive Sponsor is to carry out an assessment of the overall state of change readiness of the organization and to ensure that any barriers to successful transformation are identified and removed.

As discussed earlier, successful transformation requires a holistic approach in which an organization's culture, systems and processes are realigned as necessary to support the implementation of the transformation and the organization's ability to achieve and sustain the desired transformation objectives.

There is an initial need, therefore, to investigate whether the organizational culture and systems are aligned with one another and with the desired transformation objectives, and to address any potential organizational barriers to successful change.

This preparatory stage is especially important for the following reasons:

- To minimize the likelihood of employee resistance to the transformation
- To ensure that the organization has the necessary resources as well as the commitment among organizational leaders and employees, to actually implement the desired changes once the initial transformation project is complete
- To ensure that the organizational culture and systems are not likely to hinder a successful transformation and take steps to identify any necessary changes.

TRANSFORMATION – THE ROLE OF THE EXECUTIVE SPONSOR

The Executive Sponsor should, therefore, oversee a change-readiness assessment of both corporate culture and organizational systems and processes.

This requires an art and science-based approach, drawing on systematic methods and expertise as well as soft skills and right-brain thinking to identify any potential organizational barriers to transformation and how these might be overcome.

Cultural change initiatives as discussed in Chapter 3 should then be developed and implemented as necessary to improve the cultural change readiness of the organization.

Culture change is also promoted by modifying the seven "systemic change-shaping levers" discussed in Chapter 3, to ensure that they encourage the desired new norms and behaviours.

Though the Project Manager will usually be closely involved in this work, developing and overseeing a change-readiness assessment and implementing the results will generally require Executive-level leadership and thus falls within the Executive Sponsor's role.

The Executive Sponsor will typically focus on higher-level change strategies, which will include:

- Overseeing the overall change-readiness assessment and resulting program of change initiatives, to ensure that these meet the requirements of the transformation
- Communicating with and engaging corporate executives in the transformation initiative to establish Executive-level norms that will have a "trickle down" effect throughout the organization
- Overseeing changes to corporate-wide "systemic change-shaping levers" in collaboration with the Human Resource department.

In contrast, the responsibilities of the Project Manager with regard to change readiness are likely to include:

- Developing a cultural readiness assessment strategy and implementing data collection processes and tools
- Analyzing and reporting on the change-readiness assessment data, or overseeing this work
- Developing specific strategies and plans for improving cultural change readiness, in collaboration with the Executive Sponsor and relevant functional areas of the organization
- Developing and implementing monitoring systems to measure cultural change
- Overseeing and monitoring the impacts of specific cultural change initiatives

PROJECT GOVERNANCE

Project governance is arguably the most important role of the Executive Sponsor in organizational transformation since this is what ensures that the initiative is implemented in ways that enable it to achieve its strategic transformation objectives.

The Executive Sponsor has four specific responsibilities relating to project governance:

- Establishing a strong governance structure and effective processes
- Ensuring that the project is executed to high standards of ethics, transparency and accountability
- Ensuring that the interests of relevant stakeholders are represented in the initiative
- Ensuring that stakeholders are kept adequately informed of project progress and consulted as necessary

Governance has been defined in general terms as "the system by which companies are directed and controlled" (Cadbury Committee, 1992).

Similarly, governance of a transformation initiative involves

TRANSFORMATION – THE ROLE OF THE EXECUTIVE SPONSOR

implementing and using systems to direct and control the initiative to ensure it can meet its strategic objectives.

The main tool through which a transformation project is governed is the project Steering Committee, along with the decision-making and communications processes that are established for use by this Committee.

The Committee represents the interests of the organization as a whole in relation to the transformation and is accountable to the CEO and other corporate executives for its success.

The Executive Sponsor has multiple roles and responsibilities relating to this body:

- First, the Executive Sponsor is responsible for ensuring that a Steering Committee is established and that its membership represents the stakeholder groups or areas of the organization affected by or involved in the project.
- The Executive Sponsor then becomes formally accountable to the Steering Committee for project performance and goal achievement, and should ensure that the Committee is kept informed of project progress and consulted as necessary regarding key decisions.
- Often, the Executive Sponsor will act as Chair of the Steering Committee though this position may be occupied by another individual such as the CEO or the Project Manager, depending on the scale and importance of the transformation project.
- The specific composition of the Steering Committee will depend on the nature and complexity of the project, but for a major transformation it will often be comprised of senior representatives from the different areas of the organization that are actively involved in the initiative, such as departmental heads or their nominated representatives.

THE ART AND SCIENCE OF GOOD PRACTICE GOVERNANCE

Good-practice governance guidelines have been published within various industry sectors. One such industry example is the healthcare sector (e.g. Canada's OHA Guide to Good Governance). However, just as Project Management guidelines focus on the science of project management, these guidelines tend to focus on the science of governance rather than the art, or the people-related factors.

Best practice governance demands the use of formal, systematic methods and structures for decision-making and performance monitoring, to provide concrete evidence that a project is being well managed and can achieve its strategic transformation goals as well as its operational goals. These include, for example, the use of risk-management methods, stakeholder-management techniques and problem-solving strategies.

But the art and science approach to transformation, which we know to be crucial for successful organizational change, also requires the application of softer skills within governance, such as strong leadership, sound judgment, excellent interpersonal skills and the ability to reach a consensus and a shared vision within the Steering Committee.

Even at a corporate rather than project level, governance is often a weak link that has adverse organizational consequences.

The left-hand column of Table 10 sets out some common deficiencies in the people-related aspects of governance, relating for example to ways of thinking and interacting within the group, and the cultural factors that influence these.

The right-hand column sets out the corresponding good practices, which the Executive Sponsor of a transformation initiative should aim to implement within the project Steering Committee.

TRANSFORMATION – THE ROLE OF THE EXECUTIVE SPONSOR

Poor Governance Practices	Good Governance Practices
Disproportionate time spent on items of trivial scope	Focused only on high-level issues, with others delegated to relevant managers
Being too focused on day-to-day issues or items with a near-term focus	Having a long-term focus, while staying aware of important shorter-term factors
Being inwardly focused and not responsive enough to the external environment	Being constantly aware of the external environment and responding appropriately to external factors
Emphasis on urgent rather than important	Emphasis on important rather than urgent
Being reactive rather than proactive	Being highly proactive in identifying and dealing with important issues, while reacting in a timely way to unanticipated issues
Excessively monitoring the work of organizational members	Setting high levels of empowerment and accountability, with monitoring based on agreed performance indicators
Preferring to avoid dissent	Seeing value in dissent as a vehicle for organizational learning and improvement
Lack of shared governance goals and standards	Explicit and agreed goals and standards for governance
Lack of shared understanding of the scope of authority and responsibility	Shared understanding of scope of authority and responsibility

Table 10: Good Practice and Poor Practice in Project Governance

For an effective art and science based approach to good governance, the Executive Sponsor must specifically ensure that certain critical success factors are in place when establishing the Steering Committee for the project, as shown in Table 11.

These are based on a review of best-practice governance guidelines as well as our art- and science-based approach to successful organizational transformation.

Science-Related Critical Success Factors	Art-Related Critical Success Factors
<ul><li>The role and responsibilities of the Steering Committee and its individual members are clearly defined</li><li>The group uses a strategic approach, clear goals and a well-defined planning and implementation process</li><li>Steering Committee members are selected through a systematic, fair and transparent process</li><li>Formal processes are used to ensure full disclosure and transparency of financial, operational and quality-performance data relating to the project.</li><li>There are processes in place to ensure that conflicts of interest are avoided or managed</li><li>Established processes are in place for communicating with and seeking input from the wider organizational community</li></ul>	<ul><li>Steering Committee members have an instinctive understanding of the strategies and resources needed for an effective transformation</li><li>Steering Committee members understand and consistently work towards the strategic transformation objectives.</li><li>There is a culture of transparency and honesty</li><li>There is a good awareness and understanding of stakeholder interests and concerns regarding the transformation</li><li>The right tone is used for communicating with various organizational groups</li><li>The Steering Committee members are able to engage, influence, inspire and guide others</li><li>The Committee operates with shared beliefs,</li></ul>

Science-Related Critical Success Factors	Art-Related Critical Success Factors
■ Personal development activities are undertaken if necessary to improve members' abilities to contribute to governance of the project	attitudes, values and expectations while allowing for different viewpoints to be considered ■ There is an openness to different views and perspectives and a constructive approach to resolving conflict ■ Committee members exhibit self-awareness and a willingness to acknowledge and address their own limitations, e.g. by professional development

Table 11: Art- and Science-Related Critical Success Factors in Project Governance

To achieve these critical success factors, the Steering Committee members will need to:

- Understand and engage with the strategic objectives of the transformation initiative;
- Understand their own roles and responsibilities with regard to project governance;
- Receive clear, accurate and timely information to enable them to contribute to decision-making and meet their governance responsibilities;
- Follow transparent processes in their project-related communications and actions;
- Have a common vision for the transformation, based on a shared purpose, values and goals;
- Be prepared to engage in constructive debate and consensus building;

- Follow a clearly defined process for resolving conflicting positions or information discrepancies; and
- Be willing to revise the transformation strategy and plans if necessary to achieve the desired transformation objectives

The central role of the Executive Sponsor in project governance, therefore, is to facilitate this by establishing the necessary structure and processes and promoting an appropriate cultural climate within the Steering Committee.

The Problem of Poor Governance – Case Study

> In one consulting engagement, Schroeder & Schroeder Inc. was commissioned to evaluate a Canadian healthcare organization's governance arrangements following a merger of several hospitals.
>
> We found that despite following best-practice guidance as set out in the OHA Guide to Good Governance, there had been various shortcomings in the areas of stakeholder involvement, transparency of governance processes and decision-making and communications.
>
> This had resulted in considerable suspicion about the motives underlying the merger, concerns about perceived inequalities in the distribution of resources, and low levels of staff commitment to the newly merged organization.
>
> We recommended an art and science based approach to governance to help overcome these difficulties, incorporating a more open engagement style with high levels of stakeholder participation in decision-making; implementing a culture of transparency, with Board meeting minutes and "balanced scorecard" performance reports widely publicized, and the implication of a skills-based system of determining Board membership.

Achieving the Strategic Transformation Objectives

The final main component of the Executive Sponsor's role in a transformation initiative is to ensure that it achieves its strategic transformation objectives.

One of the most common reasons why transformation projects do not deliver business value is the failure to set project goals that are properly aligned with the core transformation objectives of the initiative. This often results in a rigid project management focus on achieving time and cost-related project goals rather than on delivering business value to the organization.

- In a project management survey conducted by KPMG New Zealand, more than half of all respondents surveyed reported that their projects were not aligned with corporate strategy, and only a third indicated that they always prepared a project business case (KPMG, 2010).
- In the business literature, a project has been conceptualized as a "temporary organization" established for the purpose of carrying out an assignment that will advance the progress of the permanent, "base" organization. From this perspective, the role of the Project Manager is to ensure that the project, as a discrete "organization" established for a specific and time-limited purpose, meets its specified time, cost and quality goals (Andersen, 2012).

The problem with this approach is that it fails to recognize that a project exists in a dynamic, constantly changing environment in which new risks and opportunities relating to the organizational transformation are continually emerging. The project is not a discrete entity but one which is necessarily closely integrated with the wider organization and which needs to evolve in ways that ensure the ultimate transformation objectives can be achieved.

This is one of the main reasons why a transformation Project Manager requires a good combination of art and science skills.

Whereas small, simple projects can often be successfully executed using formal project management tools and methods, complex transformation projects also draw heavily on the types of art-related personal skills and attributes that enable the Project Manager to identify and respond to changes in the project environment and ensure that the project remains on track to achieve its ultimate transformation goals. These types of attributes or skills are sometimes referred by terms such as business acumen, political acumen and people acumen.

Nevertheless, the Project Manager's main formal responsibility is the achievement of the project's performance goals. Should developments in the project environment mean that these are no longer aligned with the core objectives of the transformation then these performance goals should be modified accordingly so that the Project Manager is always working towards the core transformation objectives.

The Executive Sponsor, on the other hand, has a primary responsibility to ensure that the initiative achieves its core transformation objectives and it is the person in this role, rather than the Project Manager, that should be held accountable for this. This is important because ensuring that a project can achieve its transformation objectives often requires actions that fall outside the scope of the Project Manager's responsibility or power, such as negotiating with or influencing senior stakeholders, or authorizing additional resources for the project. The Project Manager cannot, therefore, be held formally accountable for the success or failure of the project to meet its ultimate transformation goals, only for performance against specified project goals (and the related organizational strategic and operational performance improvement objectives).

In the following sub-sections, we highlight some of the specific responsibilities of the Executive Sponsor that relate to the achieving the strategic transformation goals of the initiative.

Setting Project Goals

The Executive Sponsor will play an important role in ensuring that project goals properly reflect the ultimate business objectives of the transformation and are also aligned with the organization's core values and purpose. The importance of aligning any business strategy with an organization's value and purpose is discussed in our "Organizational Purpose and Transformation" White Paper, along with guidance on how to identify and formalize these to ensure that they are effective business and transformation tools.

First, the Executive Sponsor should work with the Project Manager to define performance goals for the project that reflect the core business objectives of the transformation. Table 11 shows examples of performance goals and the corresponding business objective, for a project involving the implementation of a new enterprise information system. It should be noted that the performance goals should be subsequently broken down into specific tasks, with target completion dates and costs.

Ideally, the Project Manager should take the lead in drafting the project goals and associated tasks, ensuring that he/she is familiar with the business objectives and connects the project goals with these business objectives. In this way, they will be encouraged to take ownership of the goals from an early stage. They will also be able to apply their specialist expertise to the design of realistic and measurable goals and to estimating the time and resources necessary to achieve them.

Example Project Performance Goals	Related Business Transformation Objective
• Implement and complete trial of Enterprise Information System within one department.	• To provide more robust and up-to-date evidence for management decision-making, so that strategic and operational objectives can

Example Project Performance Goals	Related Business Transformation Objective
• Develop a template for management reporting of key operational data from the EIS. • Generate trial reports, seek feedback from a sample of managers on content and format, and refine analysis and reporting system accordingly. • Complete training in the use of the EIS for all staff by specified date. • Roll out the EIS to all departments by specified date. • Collect feedback from a sample of users and refine the system	be achieved more efficiently and cost-effectively

Table 11: Example Project Performance Goals and Corresponding Transformation Objective

LINKING THE PROJECT WITH THE ORGANIZATION

To achieve the transformation goals will often require the support and contributions of many senior organizational stakeholders over which the Project Manager has little influence or authority. This is particularly the case when multiple departments or organizations are involved in the project, as is now common in major organizational transformations.

The other key role of the Executive Sponsor with regard to achieving the transformation objectives, therefore, is to act as the Executive-level connector and facilitator, ensuring that relevant senior stakeholders are aware of their own roles and responsibilities with regard to the project and, in turn, representing their interests and perspectives to the Project Manager so that these are adequately incorporated in project plans and budgets.

The Executive Sponsor role will often involve interacting with senior stakeholders to obtain the necessary resources for the transformation – especially the staffing and time inputs needed to support the implementation of the project in their own areas of the organization.

Until the transformation becomes embedded in organizational culture and systems, the Executive Sponsor will often need to draw heavily on art-related skills such as negotiation and persuasion in order to secure these resources, especially in the face of competing demands.

The Executive Sponsor will also often be required to reconcile or manage stakeholder perspectives or interests in order to deliver benefits to the organization as a whole. For example, a transformation may involve downsizing or rationalization, which benefits the organization but results in the closure of some departments.

The Executive Sponsor should ensure that relevant departmental heads have the support and resources they need to manage the changes resulting from the transformation initiative, a role which generally falls outside the scope of the Project Manager's responsibility and accountability.

In this way, the Executive Sponsor forms the main link between the project Steering Committee (representing the organization as a whole) and the day-to-day management of the transformation initiative.

A key responsibility of the Executive Sponsor is ensuring that the project reflects the Committee's priorities and decisions regarding business strategy and goals and that key developments or important issues are reported to the Committee. This is important in ensuring that the project remains aligned with the core transformation goals, and that it is able to secure the necessary inputs and resources to achieve its operational goals.

Monitoring Performance

In order to meet their responsibility of ensuring a project can meet its core transformation objectives, the Executive Sponsor needs to be able to monitor its progress against defined goals. This is also important in order to generate ROI information, justify the resources necessary for a holistic, art- and science-based transformation, and promote support for the changes at all levels of the organization.

> A recent study found that almost two-thirds of companies surveyed made no attempt to measure the return on investment of their projects and more than a quarter did not conduct any type of strategic review of the resulting benefits to the business (KPMG, 2010).
>
> Published research on company mergers has shown that the most effective of these transformations involve quantitative and qualitative monitoring of integration performance, including measures of customer satisfaction and employee engagement. However, most of the companies surveyed were not using any performance indicators to systematically measure their integration performance (Pricewaterhouse Coopers, 2009).

A transformation project has two distinct sets of goals against which progress should continually be measured:

1. Project performance goals, i.e. relating to time, cost and specific or short-term outputs or outcomes, like the examples given in the left-hand column of Table 11.
2. Business transformation goals, based on the desired organizational outcomes, such as improvements in productivity, efficiency or cost-effectiveness.

TRANSFORMATION – THE ROLE OF THE EXECUTIVE SPONSOR

The Project Manager and the Executive Sponsor should work together to define both sets of goals for the project. The Executive Sponsor will need to ensure that they are properly aligned with one another and reflect the ultimate business objectives of the transformation. The Project Manager will apply their specialist skills and expertise in ensuring that the goals are achievable, realistic and measurable.

Developing indicators for the purpose of monitoring progress is often relatively straightforward in the case of performance goals that can be measured quantitatively, for example using completion dates, the percentage of a task completed, numbers of employees using a new system of working etc.

In contrast, measuring performance against transformation objectives will often require the use of qualitative as well as quantitative indicators. For example, an assessment of the impact of a new EIS on organizational decision-making might include the collection of specific examples of changes in decision-making processes or in business strategy, collected from in-depth interviews with executives and managers.

Monitoring systems should be put in place at the outset of the project to ensure that relevant data is collected to measure progress against these indicators, and templates developed for reporting purposes, which might perhaps take the Dashboard format commonly used for management reporting.

Monitoring and reporting on the project's performance goals are a core responsibility of the Project Manager, with reports submitted to the Executive Sponsor and the Project Steering Committee according to the project plan.

These performance reports enable the Executive Sponsor to ensure that the project remains on track in meeting its transformation goals and, in consultation with the Steering Committee, to determine the need for corrective action at the project or organizational level, including the securing of needed resources.

The main responsibility for monitoring and reporting to the Project Steering Committee and other executives on progress against the transformation goals belongs to the Executive Sponsor, who is accountable for meeting these goals. The Project Manager will need to be closely involved in this, contributing the required project performance data and helping the Executive Sponsor to design and implement monitoring and reporting mechanisms.

However, generating such data for reliable assessments of the project's business impacts may also require the involvement or assistance of other functional areas such as the Business Strategy team, HR or the Communications Department. An important responsibility of the Executive Sponsor is to secure and co-ordinate these inputs at a senior level.

One of the related main roles of the Executive Sponsor is to set the pace of the transformation. This is based not only on the urgency of the desired changes – as dictated by business imperatives - but also the state of change readiness and the extent of work needed to improve this, within the context of the organization's ability to respond in an effective and constructive fashion.

Since the Project Manager will often be focused on progressing the transformation as quickly as possible to achieve targeted operational goals, the Executive Sponsor's role is important to ensure that the right balance is achieved between the speed and long-term value of the project. A transformation that is completed too quickly, without an accompanying cultural transformation, is unlikely to be sustained in the longer term.

To balance speed and sustainability requires that the Executive Sponsor has an astute understanding of the existing corporate culture and the likely willingness of the CEO and other executives to allocate resources to cultural change initiatives, and the ability to engage and negotiate with them to secure this support.

Art and Science Skills in Executive Sponsorship

Throughout this book, we have stressed the importance of an art- and science-based approach to organizational transformation, reflecting this in our discussions of the Executive Sponsor's role and in the complementary role of the Project Manager.

In this section, we provide more specific examples of the types of art and science skills that Executive Sponsors need in order to successfully carry out their roles in organizational transformation, and contrast these with the art and science skills generally required by transformation Project Managers.

The types of factors that require the Executive Sponsor to apply excellent art skills include:

- The need to understand organizational "politics" and how these affect stakeholder perspectives and interests in a project and their likelihood of being co-operative
- The need to negotiate with stakeholders and reconcile conflicting interests in the transformation
- The importance of excellent communication skills in order to represent the project effectively to internal and external stakeholders at differing levels of seniority
- The importance of understanding the full range of project opportunities and risks, including qualitative factors relating to culture and people
- The importance of forming effective relationships and connections with stakeholders to secure the input and resources necessary for project success
- The importance of staying focused on desired project outcomes and applying courage and determination in order to overcome barriers to their achievement
- The need to be able to motivate and inspire the Project Manager and their team
- The ability to apply a holistic mindset to the transformation

These factors require Executive Sponsors of organizational transformation projects to possess outstanding art-related skills and the ability to apply right-brain thinking and a holistic approach to project sponsorship.

Some of the most important art skills involved in Executive Sponsorship of a transformation include:

- Strong leadership, and the ability to inspire and motivate others
- The ability to delegate work and empower others
- The ability to inspire trust, in order to overcome resistance and secure the necessary involvement and inputs from organizational members.
- Excellent interpersonal / communication skills to interact with a range of stakeholders
- Good negotiating and persuasion skills to secure resources and support for the project
- Political and business acumen to identify project risks and opportunities
- Good negotiating and persuasion skills to secure resources and support for the project
- Political and business acumen to identify project risks and opportunities
- The ability to remain focused on "the big picture" and ultimate objectives of the transformation

However, science-related skills and the ability to apply left-brain thinking are also increasingly important requirements of the Executive Sponsors of major organizational transformations.

The types of factors that require science skills on the part of the Executive Sponsor include:

- The need for a broad awareness of project management methods and techniques, in order to understand and interpret project plans, budgets, work breakdown schedules,

etc. and to communicate effectively with the Project Manager;
- The importance of being able to understand and interpret quantitative performance indicators; and
- The importance of implementing a systematic approach to project governance.

Related to these, some of the most important science skills in Executive Sponsorship include:

- Understanding the importance of a systematic approach to transformation management;
- Having adequate knowledge of project management tools and methodologies, to support and advise the Project Manager in their work; and
- Having an excellent knowledge of and ability to implement best-practice project governance structures and processes.

SUMMARY

The Executive Sponsor of a transformation is important on a number of fronts.

Organizational transformation projects are often highly complex, involving multiple organizations, dispersed teams and numerous stakeholders with different and sometimes conflicting interests. As a result, many things need to be achieved which fall outside the authority and control of the transformation Project Manager, such as negotiating with senior organizational stakeholders.

The Executive Sponsor therefore plays an important connecting and facilitating role in the transformation and is responsible for ensuring that the strategic transformation objectives are met.

The Executive Sponsor is also primarily responsible for establishing a strong governance structure and processes for the transformation project and ensuring the overall organization is prepared for a successful transformation.

Accordingly, the Executive Sponsor has four specific responsibilities relating to project governance:

- Establishing a strong governance structure and effective processes
- Ensuring that the project is executed to high standards of ethics, transparency and accountability
- Ensuring that the interests of relevant stakeholders are represented in the initiative
- Ensuring that stakeholders are kept adequately informed of project progress and consulted as necessary

Overall, the Executive Sponsor has two main responsibilities in preparing the organization for transformation:

- Selection of the Project Manager: This involves determining the types and balance of art and science skills needed for the transformation project, ensuring that appropriate skills assessment methods and tools are in place, and overseeing the P selection process to ensure the right person for the job is appointed.
- Assessing organizational change readiness, which involves investigating the change readiness of the organization's people and culture as well as its processes and infrastructure. This is important so that potential barriers to an art and science based transformation can be addressed, and to help ensure that the intended transformation objectives can actually be achieved.

The Executive Sponsor acts as an important link between the project and the whole organization, providing support in areas where the Project Manager has little or no authority, as well as senior-level strategic input to keep the project on track.

TRANSFORMATION – THE ROLE OF THE EXECUTIVE SPONSOR

Specific responsibilities include:

- Ensuring that project goals properly reflect the ultimate business objectives of the transformation and are also aligned with the organization's core values and purpose.
- Acting as the executive-level connector and facilitator, to ensure that relevant senior stakeholders are aware of their own roles and responsibilities with regard to the project and representing their interests and perspectives to the Project Manager.
- If necessary, reconciling or managing conflicting stakeholder perspectives or interests in order to deliver benefits for the organization as a whole.
- Monitoring and evaluating project progress against the strategic transformation goals.

Throughout the book, we have emphasized the importance of an "art- and science"-based approach to transformation management and of adequately preparing the organization to undertake a major change initiative. In the penultimate chapter, some specific tools developed by Schroeder & Schroeder Inc. to facilitate this process are discussed, to provide further practical guidance on how change readiness can be assessed and improved in order to maximize the likelihood of a successful transformation.

TRANSFORMATION ASSESSMENT SYSTEMS AND TOOLS

Transformation assessment systems and tools are important to ensure that all possible risks to a successful transformation are addressed and that the potential for a highly successful organizational initiative, that delivers the intended strategic and operational performance objectives, is maximized.

These should be designed from an art and science perspective in order to truly enhance an organization's ability to effectively transform. This means incorporating both quantitative and qualitative measures and using a holistic, "right- and left-brain" approach when designing the assessment tools and analyzing the data generated.

In this chapter, we provide examples of three "art- and science"-based systems and tools designed to improve an management of a transformation initiative.

These consist of:

- The Project Management Assessment System™ (PMAS™)
- The Organizational Change Readiness Assessment System™ (OCRAS™)
- The Post Project Assessment System™ (PPAS™)

Project Manager Assessment System™ (PMAS™)

The Project Manager Assessment System™ (PMAS™) was created for the purpose of evaluating and identifying required improvements to an organization's project management function.

PMAS™ was developed on the basis of an analysis of published project management skill frameworks, an extensive literature review and more than a quarter century of practical experience which has enabled Schroeder & Schroeder, Inc. to identify the art and science skills most critical to effective project management.

This system uses a multi-methods approach to assessing Project Managers not only in terms of their knowledge and skills but also on their ability to apply these effectively to the different types of project management, including the management of major organizational transformations.

Initially, the art- and science-related skills, abilities and experience of individual Project Managers and others with project management responsibilities within the organization are investigated using a number of different methods of data collection and analysis, including in-depth interviews, an online self-completion survey and 360-degree assessment.

By triangulating data from various sources, an organization using this system can achieve a robust and reliable assessment of each individual's art and science skills; allocate Project Managers to roles in which their skills and expertise can best contribute to the transformation objectives and identify areas for skills development.

The results of the individual assessments are then collated to provide a comprehensive overview of the state of the current project management function across the organization, or at the team or departmental level. An example of a graphical output from the PMAS™ is shown in Figure 7.

TRANSFORMATION ASSESSMENT SYSTEMS AND TOOLS

The holistic tool can be customized to the needs of individual organizations, and can be used to develop tailored recommendations and a proposed action plan for the enhancement of the project management function for more effective transformation management.

From the synthesis of the results at the team, departmental or organizational level, the organization can identify overall strengths and weaknesses in its project management function and take measures to improve this before a major transformation project goes ahead.

The overall outcome is a clear roadmap for the enhancement of the project management function in order to reduce the risks of transformation and other organizational projects, improve the efficiency and effectiveness of project management and generate positive business impacts.

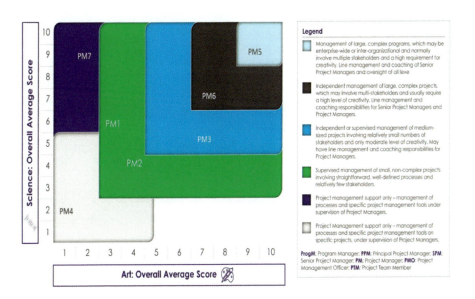

Figure 7: Example PMAS^{TM} Output

ORGANIZATIONAL CHANGE READINESS ASSESSMENT SYSTEM™ (OCRAS™)

Like the PMAS™, Schroeder & Schroeder Inc.'s Organizational Change Readiness Assessment System ™ (OCRAS™) is based on a multi-methods approach to data collection and analysis in order to ensure that all possible risks to successful transformation are addressed. It includes a systematic review of organizational structure and relevant company documents as well as in-depth interviews with a range of key stakeholders throughout the organization and has two main parts.

As we have discussed in this paper, successful transformation requires a holistic approach in which an organization's culture, systems and processes are realigned as necessary to support the implementation of the transformation and the organization's ability to achieve and sustain the desired transformation objectives.

The first stage of the OCRAS™ involves a systematic review of the organizational structure and systems, as well as documentation and interviews with senior stakeholders. This is intended to generate an understanding of change readiness in relation to the seven systemic "change- shaping levers", which include the leadership system, the compensation and rewards system, the approach to performance management and the communications system and tools (Figure 4).

It is crucial to ensure that these systems promote the types of attitudes and behaviour that will support transformation per se, as well as the achievement of the specific project goals, and are not likely to hinder the transformation in any way.

The cultural change-readiness component of the OCRAS™ consists of an organizational climate assessment survey and in-depth interviews with a diverse sample of organizational members and other stakeholders. This explores aspects of corporate culture and other people-related factors likely to promote or hinder successful transformation, such as leadership styles, employee morale and the perceived expectations of and risks relating to the proposed changes.

The OCRAS™ uses advanced analytics to identify and prioritize drivers of change success, and qualitative data collection and analysis intended to provide insights beyond the "hard" data about how best to prepare the organization and its culture for effective transformation. Some example outputs are shown in Figure 8.

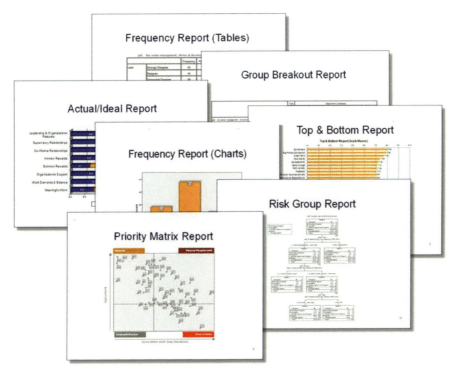

Figure 8: Sample OCRAS™ Outputs

The two components of the OCRAS™ are closely inter-related and require the application of both art and science to understand and influence the impacts of organizational systems and corporate culture on transformation.

In general terms, however:

- The first stage of the change-readiness assessment is predominantly science-based, requiring a systematic,

PREPARING FOR ORGANIZATIONAL TRANSFORMATION

methodological approach to analyzing organizational systems and their effects.

- The cultural change-readiness component is predominantly art-based, requiring an astute understanding of how and why people think and act in certain ways, and how to influence this in ways that will help promote successful transformation.

POST PROJECT ASSESSMENT SYSTEM™

The ongoing or frequent nature of organizational transformation in today's business environment strongly indicates that in order to excel at art- and science-based transformation, companies should implement systems for learning from experience. In particular, they should document the experiential lessons and tacit knowledge generated from each project, and ensure that this material is widely disseminated and shared, especially among Project Managers.

Schroeder & Schroeder Inc.'s Post Project Assessment System™ (PPAS™) was developed in order to capture key lessons relating to project performance in relation to the art and science skills identified in our Project Manager Assessment System™ (PMAS™), taking into account the nature of the project and its skill requirements. The system has also been designed to reflect best-practice principles of project assessment identified from an extensive review of the project management literature and published guidance and our proprietary Art and Science of Transformation® approach.

Like our other assessment tools, the PPAS™ is based on mixed methods of collecting both quantitative and qualitative data in order to provide an "art- and science"-based, holistic understanding of project management performance and areas for improvement. Quantitative measures of project performance are collected using a questionnaire in which project team members rank the importance of specified art and science skills to the project as a whole and to their own role on the project. They are then asked to assess their own

TRANSFORMATION ASSESSMENT SYSTEMS AND TOOLS

performance and that of the project team against each of the identified art and science skills. Follow-up qualitative interviews are conducted to help explain the survey findings and to provide additional material on project experiences for use in improving the organization's future transformation management performance.

BUSINESS BENEFITS OF ASSESSMENT TOOLS

Using the types of tools described in this chapter can significantly improve an organization's ability to undergo successful transformation and achieve the desired business benefits. Further, there are many potential spin-off benefits of using these art- and science-based tools and systems, which include, for example:

- Reduced business risk – projects can be implemented with confidence, in the knowledge that project and program managers are well equipped to deliver positive outcomes.
- Cost-effective staffing – selection and deployment of Project and Program Managers will be more effective and efficient.
- Higher return on training investment – organizations will be better equipped to develop training and development plans that are closely aligned with business and project goals.
- Maximum utilization of skill sets – Under-utilized skills and expertise will come to light, which can be usefully employed in improving the business.
- Enhanced overall project management – specific strengths and weaknesses in project management can be identified, and a clear roadmap developed for the improvement of the project management function.
- Better alignment of organizational culture with business objectives – it will be possible to identify the cultural changes necessary to help ensure that organizational members think and behave in ways that contribute to the achievement of business goals.

- Efficient and effective organizational systems – it will become clear how systems and processes reinforce organizational culture, and how to redesign these to promote the changes necessary to support transformation and goal achievement.
- Ability to measure ROI and business impact – the most suitable indicators and methods for measuring the impact and value of transformations will become clearer.

SUMMARIZING THE KEY FEATURES OF THE ASSESSMENT SYSTEMS

Schroeder & Schroeder's Project Manager Assessment System™ (PMAS™) uses a multi-methods approach to assess Project Managers not only in terms of their art- and science-related knowledge and skills but also on their ability to apply these effectively to the management of major organizational transformations

The Organizational Change Readiness Assessment System™ (OCRAS™) has two main components, which address

- Cultural change readiness, and
- Alignment of the organization's "systemic change shaping levers", the human resource management systems that interact with and reinforce corporate culture by promoting certain types of behaviours.

The Post Project Assessment System™ (PPAS™) was developed in order to capture key lessons relating to project performance in relation to key art and science skills for transformation project management.

In the final chapter, we summarize the main messages of this book and make some concluding comments about the importance of preparing an organization for transformation using our recommended Art and Science of Transformation® approach.

SUMMARY AND CONCLUSION

As this paper has highlighted, organizations of all types now need to continually transform in order to remain competitive and efficient. The nature as well as the frequency of organizational transformation projects has been changing in recent years, with new demands on the Project Management function.

In particular, there is increasing evidence that successful transformations require far more than conventional project management skills; management of the people involved in the transformation has become even more important in determining the success or failure of these types of initiatives, and a transformation Project Manager is now more likely than ever to be involved in core business planning and strategy development.

The complex, multi-stakeholder nature of most major transformation projects has also elevated the role and importance of another key organizational player: the Executive Sponsor of the transformation who acts as the link between the transformation project and the wider organization. An effective partnership between the Project Manager and the Executive Sponsor has become one of the critical success factors in transformation, as well as the ability of both the Project Manager and the Executive Sponsor to effectively carry out their respective roles and responsibilities using an art- and science-based approach. Another critical success factor in organizational transformation is good governance, which is also a key role of the Executive Sponsor of a transformation project.

Schroeder & Schroeder's Art and Science of Transformation® framework was developed in recognition that conventional project management training and standards are inadequate in today's business environment, in which transformation projects are increasingly large and complex and involve a wide range of stakeholders.

Our extensive research and first-hand consulting experience have demonstrated the importance of an art- and science-based approach to transformation which recognizes the central role of people-related factors in driving or hindering change and combines this with best-practice project management techniques and methods.

Since most project management training bodies have not yet responded effectively to the new transformation management requirements, firms must take responsibility for ensuring that their own project management function and organizational environments are adequately prepared to support frequent transformation.

This entails responding and adapting as necessary to the rapidly changing environment and the risks and opportunities that arise. In particular, there is a need to ensure that the right skills, expertise and mindsets are in place for a strategic and holistic approach to organizational change.

In this book, we have focused primarily on the roles of the Project Manager and the Executive Sponsor in the context of a single transformation. However, the content is equally relevant for organizational leaders and managers more generally, who need to ensure that the organizational environment, in general, is supportive of and promotes transformation and that any specific barriers to change, whether cultural or systemic in nature, are removed before

SUMMARY AND CONCLUSION

costly transformation projects are implemented. The types of assessment systems described in Chapter 8 are useful tools for evaluating an organization's readiness for transformation per se, in addition to the specific skills and expertise needed for a particular transformation initiative.

More generally, to enhance an organization's ability to successfully transform, organizational leaders need to:

- Ensure that the appropriate type of project management expertise is in place
- Ensure that the organizational environment is supportive of an art- and science -based transformation.
- Encourage experiential organizational learning and the development of a knowledge base of effective practice

For more information and advice on organizational transformation, readers may be interested in other publications available from harold@schroeder-inc.com, including a wide range of white papers on various topics relating to the Art and Science of Transformation®.

REFERENCES

Aiken, C.B. & Keller, S.P. (2007). *The CEO's role in leading transformation.* McKinsey & Company. Retrieved from http://www.mckinsey.com/insights/organization/the_ceos_role_in_leading_transformation

Alam, M., Gale, A., Brown, M., Khan, A. (2010). The importance of human skills in project management professional development. *International Journal of Managing Projects in Business, 3*(3): 495-516.

Andersen, E.S. (2008), Rethinking project management: An organisational perspective. Prentice-Hall, Harlow.

Andersen, E.S. (2012). Illuminating the role of the project owner. *International Journal of Managing Projects in Business, 5*(1): 67-85.

Anderson, D. & Anderson, L.A. (n.d.). *What is transformation, and why is it so hard to manage?* Retrieved from http://changeleadersnetwork.com/free-resources/what-is-transformation-and-why-is-it-so-hard-to-manage#sthash.tVj4wbC0.s6EH8GMf.dpuf

Apfel, A., Light, M., Handler, R.A. et al., (2010). Predicts 2011: PPM goes from managing projects to managing value and change. Gartner Research.

Association for Project Management (2012). APM Body of Knowledge 6th edition. Author.

Batkins, S. (2013). *The paperworkers: Examining trends in regulatory specialist employment.* American Action Forum. Retrieved from http://americanactionforum.org/research/the-paperworkers-examining-trends-in-regulatory-specialist-employment

Bloch, M., Blumberg, S. & and Laartz, J. (2012). *Delivering large-scale IT projects on time, on budget and on value.* McKinsey & Company. Retrieved from http://www.mckinsey.com/insights/business_technology/delivering_large-scale_it_projects_on_time_on_budget_and_on_value

Bradt, G. (2013, August 28). *The right way to divide responsibilities between chairman and CEO.* Forbes [online]. Retrieved from http://www.forbes.com/sites/georgebradt/2013/08/28/the-right-way-to-divide-responsibilities-between-chairman-and-ceo/

Bredin, K. and Soderlund, J. (2003), Svenska projekts overview of education 2003: An overview of contemporary education within the areas of project management and project organization at Swedish universities, Svenska Projekt, Stockholm.

Brown, K, Hyer, N. & Ettenson, R. (2013). The question every project team should answer. *MIT Sloan Management Review, 55*(1): 49-57.

Burke, W.W. (2010). *Organization change: theory and practice.* Thousand Oaks, CA: Sage Publications.

Business Reporter (2013, June 6). It takes a mature organisation to cut project failure rates. *Business Reporter* [online]. Retrieved from http://business-reporter.co.uk/2013/06/it-takes-a-mature-organisation-to-cut-project-failure-rates/

Cadbury, A. (1992). The Committee on the Financial Aspects of Corporate Governance, London: Gee and Company.

REFERENCES

CapGemini (2007). *Trends in business transformation: Survey of European executives.* Retrieved from http://www.org-portal.org/fileadmin/media/legacy/Capgemini_-_Trends_in_Business_Transformation.pdf

CapGemini Consulting (2009). *Business transformation: From crisis response to radical changes that will create tomorrow's business.* Available from http://www.capgemini.com/insights-and-resources/by-publication/trends-in-business- transformation-2009/

Carbone, T.A. (2004). Project manager skills development: a survey of programs and practitioners. *Engineering Management Journal 16*(3): 7.

Cleland, D. I., & Ireland, L, R. (2008) *Project manager's handbook: Applying best practices across global industries.* New York, NY: McGraw-Hill Professional.

Cognizant (2013). Understanding failed core banking projects. Retrieved from http://www.cognizant.com/InsightsWhitepapers/Understanding-Failed-Core-Banking-Projects.pdf

Collins, J. (1995). Building companies to last. Inc. Special issue: the state of small business. Retrieved from http://www.jimcollins.com/article_topics/articles/building-companies.html

Collins, J. C. & Porras, J. I. (2005). *Built to last: Successful habits of visionary companies.* London: Random House Business Books.

Crawford, L., Morris, P., Thomas, J. and Winter, M. (2006). Practitioner development: from trained technicians to reflective practitioners. *International Journal of Project Management 24*(8): 722-733.

Crawford, L.H. & Brett, C. (2001). Exploring the role of the project sponsor. In: *Proceedings of the PMI New Zealand Annual Conference 2001: Project Success: Putting it all together.* Wellington, New Zealand: PMINZ

Datt, S. & Nash, S. (2013). Accelerating innovation in 'new normal' times. *The Journal of Government Financial Management, 62*(3), 18-22, 24-25.

Deloitte (2014). Roles and responsibilities. Retrieved from http://www.corpgov.deloitte.com/site/us/board- governance/roles-and-responsibilities/;jsessionid=myTgScQK4bv31TyZ221yybnQhhSGzRbvjQzjnLNHgSnJRpJnFysv!- 170431906!NONE

Denning, S. (2012). From maximizing shareholder value to delighting the customer. *Strategy & Leadership 40*(3), 12–16.

Dyer, S. (2006). The Root Causes of Poor Communication. *Cost Engineering, 48*(6) 8-12.

Economist Intelligence Unit (2008) *A change for the better: Steps for successful business transformation*. Retrieved from: http://viewswire.eiu.com/report_dl.asp?mode=fi&fi=1003398485.PDF

Egginton, B. (2012). Realising the benefits of investment in project management training. *International Journal of Managing Projects in Business, 5*(3), 508-527.

Fortune, J., White, D., Jugdev, K. & Walker, D. (2011). Looking again at current practice in project management. *International Journal of Managing Projects in Business, 4*(4): 553-572.

Gartner (2013). *Gartner says it's the beginning of a new era: The digital industrial economy*. Retrieved from http://www.gartner.com/newsroom/id/2602817.

Gillard, S. (2009). Soft skills and technical expertise of effective project managers. *Issues in Informing Science and Information Technology, 6*, 723-729.

Grenny, J., Maxfield, D., & Shimberg, A. (2007). How project leaders can overcome the crisis of silence. *MIT Sloan Management Review, 48*(4), 46-52.

REFERENCES

Grunfeldt, L.A. and Jakobsen, E.W. (2006), *Hvem eier Norge? Eierskap og verdiskapning i et grenseløst næringsliv,* Universitetsforlaget, Oslo.

Gulati, R., N. Nohria, and F. Wohlegezogen. 2010. Roaring out of recession. *Harvard Business Review 88*(3), 63–69.

Hahn, I., Bredillett, C., Kim, G., & Taloc, M. (2012). Agility of project manager in global IS Project. *The Journal of Computer Information Systems, 53*(2), 31-38.

Hällgren, M., Nilsson, A., Blomquist, T. & Söderholm, A, (2012). Relevance lost! A critical review of project management standardisation. *International Journal of Managing Projects in Business, 5*(3), 457-485.

Hardy-Vallee, B. (2012, February 7). The cost of bad project management. *Gallup Business Journal* [online]. Retrieved from http://businessjournal.gallup.com/content/152429/cost-bad-project-management.aspx#1

Hartman, F. (2008). Preparing the mind for dynamic management. *International Journal of Project Management 26*(3), 258-67.

Helm, J., & Remington, K. (2005). Effective project sponsorship: an evaluation of the role of the executive sponsor in complex infrastructure projects by senior project managers. *Project Management Journal, 36*(3), 51.

Hodgson, D. and Cicmil, S. (2006). Are projects real? The PMBOK® and the legitimation of project management knowledge. In Hodgson, D. and Cicmil, S. (Eds.). *Making Projects Critical,* pp. 29-50. New York: NY: Palgrave Macmillan.

IBM Corporation (2008). The enterprise of the future: IBM Global CEO Study 2008. Available from www.ibm.com/enterpriseofthefuture.

Interthink Consulting Inc. (2005). Effectively managing government projects. A discussion of the report of Ontario's Special Task Force on the Management of Large-Scale Information & Information

Technology Projects. Retrieved from http://interthink.ca/wp-content/uploads/2013/07/Interthink-White-Paper-Effectively-Managing-Government-Projects.pdf

Jackson, S., Farndale, E. & Kakabadse, A. (2003). Executive development: meeting the needs of top teams and boards. *Journal of Management Development, 22*(3), 185-265.

Janssen, M., van Veenstra, A.F. & van der Voort, H. (2013). Management and failure of large transformation projects: Factors affecting user adoption. *IFIP Advances in Information and Communication Technology, 402,* 121-135

Jarocki, T.L. (2011). The next evolution: Enhancing and unifying project and change management: The emergence one method for total project success. Princeton, NJ: Brown & Williams Publishing, LLC.

Johansen, A., Steiro, T. & Ekambaram, A. (2012). Knowledge management - What do uncertainty management and the project owner perspective have to do with it? *European Conference on Knowledge Management:* 548-XXIX. Kidmore End: Academic Conferences International Limited.

Jugdev, K. & Mathur, G. (2012). Classifying project management resources by complexity and leverage. *International Journal of Managing Projects in Business 5*(1): 105-124

Kaplan, S. (2012). The business model innovation factory: How to stay relevant when the world is changing. Hoboken, NJ: John Wiley & Sons, Inc.

Karlsen, J.T. (2010). Project owner involvement for information and knowledge sharing in uncertainty management. *International Journal of Managing Projects in Business, 3*(4): 642-660

Kloppenborg, T., Manolis, C. & Tesch, D. (2009). Successful project sponsor behaviors during project initiation: An empirical investigation. *Journal of Managerial Issues, 21*(1): 140-159.

REFERENCES

Kloppenborg, T., Tesch, D. & Manolis, C. (2011). Investigation of the sponsor's role in project planning. *Management Research Review* 34(4): 400-416.

Konstantopoulos, G. (2010). The evolution of the project manager role. *ProjectTimes*. Retrieved from http://www.projecttimes.com/articles/the-evolution-of-the-project-manager-role.html

KPMG (2010). New Zealand project management survey 2010. Retrieved from http://www.kpmg.com/NZ/en/IssuesAndInsights/ArticlesPublications/Documents/Proje ct-Management-Survey-report.pdf

KPMG New Zealand (2013). Project management survey report 2013. Retrieved from http://www.kpmg.com/NZ/en/IssuesAndInsights/ArticlesPublications/Documents/KPMG-Project- Management-Survey-2013.pdf

Labuschagne, L., Cooke-Davies, T., Crawford, L., Hobbs, B. & Remington, K. (2006). Exploring the Role of the Project Sponsor. *Proceedings of PMI Global Congress 2006-- North America.*

Lory, M. & McCalman, J. (2002). Management consultancies as brands: Can David learn from Goliath? *Journal of Brand Management* 9(6): 412-419.

Maslow, A.H. (1943) A theory of human motivation. *Psychological Review 50*: 370-396.

Maslow, A. H. (1954). *Motivation and personality.* New York: Harper and Row.

MBO Partners (2011). *Majority of Workforce Will Be Independent by 2020.* Retrieved from http://www.mbopartners.com/press-room/press-releases/majority-workforce-will-be-independent-2020-0#.UebzOw-N7Ok.email

McKinsey & Company (2010). *Global Forces: how strategic trends affect your business.* Available from www.mckinsey.com/clientservice/strategy/pdf/Strategic_Trends.pdf; Ernst & Young, op.cit.

McKinsey & Company. Creating organizational transformations: McKinsey Global Survey Results, 2008, Available at http://www.mckinseyquarterly.com/Organization/Change_Management/Creating_organizational_transformations_McKinsey_Global_Survey_results_2195.

McKinsey Global Institute (2014). *Global Flows in a Digital Age.* Retrieved from http://www.mckinsey.com/insights/globalization/global_flows_in_a_digital_age

Miller, R. & Hobbs, B. (2005). Governance regimes for large complex projects. *Project Management Journal, 36*(3), 42-50.

Morley, S. (2011). Winners and losers in the "New Normal Economy". The top 10 differences. *The American Salesman 56*(3), 10-14.

Muller, R. and Turner, R.J. (2005). The impact of principal–agent relationship and contract type on communication between project owner and manager. *International Journal of Project Management, 23*(5): 398-403.

OECD (1999, 2004) Principles of Corporate Governance. Paris: OECD.

Olsson, N.O.E., Johansen, A., Langlo, J.A., & Torp, O. (2008). Project ownership: implications on success measurement. *Measuring Business Excellence, 12*(1), 39-46.

Panwar, R., Vlosky, R., & Hansen, E. (2012). Gaining competitive advantage in the new normal. *Forest Products Journal, 62*(6), 420-428.

Pappas, L. (2005). The state of project management training. *PM Network 19*(8): 60-66.

REFERENCES

Patton, N. & Shechet, A. (2007). Wisdom for building the project manager/project sponsor relationship: Partnership for project success. *Crosstalk: The Journal of Defense Software Engineering.* November 2007.

Pollack, J. (2006). The changing paradigms of project management. *International Journal of Project Management 25*(3): 266-74.

PricewaterhouseCoopers (2014). *Good to Grow: 2014 US CEO Survey.* Retrieved from http://www.pwc.com/us/en/ceo-survey-us/2014/assets/2014-us-ceo-survey.pdf

PricewaterhouseCoopers Ltd.(2009). Post Merger Integration Survey 2009. Retrieved from http://download.pwc.com/ie/pubs/post_merger_integration_survey_2009.pdf

Project Management Institute (2004). *A Guide to the Project Management Body of Knowledge.* (PMBOK® Guide). Author.

Project Management Institute (2008). A Guide to the Project Management Body of Knowledge (PMBOK® Guide – 4th edition). Author.

Project Management Institute (2010). Program Management 2010: A study of program management in the U.S. Federal Government, PMI. June 2010. Retrieved from http://www.pmi.org/Business-Solutions/~/media/PDF/Business-Solutions/Government%20Program%20Management%20Study%20Report_FINAL.ashx

Project Management Institute (2011). PMI Pulse of the Profession Report. Author.

Project Management Institute (2013). *A Guide to the Project Management Body of Knowledge* (PMBOK® Guide – 5th edition). Author.

Project Management Institute (2013). *PMI's Pulse of the Profession*™: *The High Cost of Low Performance 2013*. Retrieved from http://www.pmi.org/Knowledge-Center/Pulse/~/media/PDF/Business-Solutions/PMI-Pulse%20Report-2013Mar4.ashx

Project Management Institute (2013). Project Management between 2010 and 2020. Retrieved from http://www.pmi.org/~/media/PDF/Business-Solutions/PMIProjectManagementSkillsGapReport.ashx

Project Management Institute (2014). *The High Cost of Low Performance 2014. PMI's Pulse of the Profession*®. Retrieved from http://www.pmi.org/~/media/PDF/Business-Solutions/PMI_Pulse_2014.ashx

Project Management Institute (n.d.). Executive Engagement: The Role of the Sponsor. PMI White Paper. http://www.pmi.org/business-solutions/~/media/PDF/Business-Solutions/Executive%20Engagement_FINAL.ashx

Ranf, D.E. (2011). Project management – then and now. Universitatis Apulensis: *Series Oeconomica, 13*(2): 596-603.

Reed, A. H., & Knight, L. V. (2013). Project duration and risk factors on virtual projects. *The Journal of Computer Information Systems 54*(1), 75-83.

Reich, B.H. and Wee, S.Y. (2006). Searching for knowledge in the PMBOK® guide. *Project Management Journal 37*: 11-26.

Savolainen, T. (2013). Change implementation in intercultural context: A case study of creating readiness to change. *Journal of Global Business Issues, 7*(2), 51-58.

Schroeder, H. (2012). Cultural transformation: The Art and Science of Transformation White Paper Series. Schroeder & Schroeder Inc.

Schroeder, H. (2013). Organizational purpose and transformation: The Art and Science of Transformation White Paper Series. Schroeder & Schroeder Inc.

REFERENCES

Smith, C. and Winter, M. (2005). The Profession and Practitioner Development: Sensemaking Paper 6, Manchester: EPSRC.

Syal, R. (2013, September 18). Abandoned NHS IT system has cost £10bn so far. *The Guardian.* Retrieved from http://www.theguardian.com/society/2013/sep/18/nhs- records-system-10bn

Taylor, D. (2013). Grow the core: How to focus on your core business for brand success. Chichester: John Wiley & Sons Ltd.

Thomas, J. & Mengel, T. (2008). Preparing project managers to deal with complexity – advanced project management education. *International Journal of Project Management 26*(3): 304-15.

Thornbury, J. (2003). Creating a living culture: The challenges for business leaders. *Corporate Governance 3*(2): 68-79.

Tuckman, B. W. (2001). Developmental sequence in small groups. *Group Facilitation, 3*, Spring, 66-81.

United Nations Economic and Social Commission for Asia and the Pacific (ESCAP). (2014). What is Good Governance? Retrieved from http://www.unescap.org/pdd/prs/ProjectActivities/Ongoing/gg/governance.asp

Vandermerwe, S. (2004). Achieving deep customer focus. *MIT Sloan Management Review, 45*(3), 26-35.

Ward, J. & Uhl, A. (2012). Success and failure in transformation: Lessons from 13 case studies. *Business Transformation Online 3*(1 February 2012). Retrieved from https://www.bta-online.com/what-we-do/360-journal/previous-issues/journal-issue-3/

Zekic, Z. & Samarzija, L. (2012). Project management of dynamic optimization of business performance. *International Business Research, 5*(12): 99-111.

Made in the USA
Charleston, SC
04 July 2016